RISKING ON PURPOSE

By Peg Flandreau West

Editorial assistance by Sue Gordon

Cover art by Nancy Livingston

September 1991

© Protective Behaviors Inc.
1005 Rutledge Street, Madison, Wisconsin, USA

©PROTECTIVE BEHAVIORS INC.(US)

Published 1991

by ESSENCE PUBLICATIONS PTY LTD
PO Box 228
Burnside, South Australia, 5066.

All rights reserved

ISBN 0 9588033 3 1

West, Peg Flandreau
Risking on Purpose

Cover art Nancy Livingston

Wholly produced in Adelaide South Australia

Book production: Essence Publications Pty Ltd and Core Text

PREFACE

On May 6th 1991 Peg Flandreau West was tragically killed in a car accident. At that time she had finished the near-final draft of this book and was working on final editing in preparation for its launch at the Fifth National Protective Behaviours Conference in Adelaide on September 7th.

Her death came as a devastating shock to all who knew and loved this amazing woman, and to many hundreds of people who had been influenced by her life and work without ever knowing her personally. The Protective Behaviours Program which she formulated and lived has been the vehicle through which countless children and adults have been able to take positive action for their own safety and that of others.

Peg West's dream was of a world without violence. This book is the story of her life and the development of the concepts on which the Protective Behaviours Program was based. The title *Risking on Purpose* aptly reflects Peg's commitment to her dream and the sense of fun and adventure which characterised both her life and her work. In addition to her own story she has included many examples of 'success stories' which have been told or sent to her by other people, young and old, who have used the strategies of Protective Behaviours to empower themselves in a variety of situations.

My own first introduction to Peg West was in May 1985, when I attended one of the first trainer-training sessions in Protective Behaviours she conducted in Australia. I had the sense even at that time that those two days were going to have a profound effect on my life. Little did I guess how profound that effect was going to be.

Part of the story of how my partner, Sandy Litt, and I set up Essence Publications has been included by Peg in Chapter 9. This was very much a 'risk on purpose' for us, and one which we would not have taken without Peg's support and encouragement. It has therefore been our great delight to work with her towards the publication of this her story, and my especial privilege to have been asked by her colleagues and family to put the final touches to the book on Peg's behalf after her death. The launch of the book will happen as planned at the Protective Behaviours National Conference, with several of Peg's friends and colleagues from Wisconsin taking part. The theme of the Conference is *Living Without Violence : Let's Talk About It*. Peg West was to have been a keynote speaker, on the theme, *Creating a Violence-Free Future - Right Now!*

It is my sincere hope, as I know it was Peg's, that reading this book will bring to its readers a sense of hope for a non-violent future, a hope that brings with it the energy and inspiration to be part of bringing that dream into reality.

Sue Gordon
Adelaide. August 1991.

APPRECIATIONS AND DEDICATION

An enormous number of people have contributed to the publication of this book, many of whom are not known to the publishers. However on Peg West's behalf we would like to express an enormous thank you to you all and especially to:

> Peg's family who supported and enabled her to become the precious gift to the world that she undoubtedly was
>
> The Board Members and Peg's colleagues in Protective Behaviors Inc (US) for having the faith in us to complete this book, and especially to Michael Biernbaum for his patience and good humour in helping us to tie up seemingly endless details
>
> The students, parents, teachers, colleagues, friends and acquaintances whose experiences assisted in the development of the Protective Behaviours concepts
>
> All those who have contributed their success stories to this book. Many of you are named herein. To those whose names we don't know, our apologies and thanks for your unsung participation in the achievement of a dream.

And on behalf of ourselves, (and we feel sure we speak for many, many others,) a thank you that cannot be adequately put into words to Peg Flandreau West herself, through whose life we have been challenged, excited, enriched and empowered.

This book is dedicated to her memory, and to the achievement of her dream of a world without violence.

Sue Gordon and Sandy Litt
Essence Publications
August 1991

INTRODUCTION

I am writing this book to share the adventure of Protective Behaviours, an adventure that I almost missed - an adventure that I almost didn't recognize, an adventure that I almost didn't allow to happen.

I'm very grateful now that I did take those risks. My life has changed dramatically as a result - and through these adventures others, too, have seen things differently. Actions based on deepening understandings and new integrations have come into being. And there's more to come. The Australian National Protective Behaviours Forum has as one of its goals 'teaching the Protective Behaviours Process to every individual in Australia as a way of enhancing world peace.'

But I'm getting ahead of the story. Back in 1975, I was three years short of fifty years old, and had been working as a school social worker for more than a decade, a job I did well and creatively - and I had aided in initiating a number of innovative projects. I often told people that it was the most interesting social work job I had ever done. My expectation was that I would continue at that job for another eight or ten years and then slip quietly into retirement. Little did I know what the world had in store for me!

I remember the beginnings clearly. One day in October 1975, though I have forgotten the exact calendar date, a colleague and I walked into a classroom of seven year olds and asked them what they knew about feeling safe. At that moment, the Protective Behaviours Process started to come into reality.

My colleague, school psychologist Joan Panepinto and I had been stewing about the situation at one of the schools where we were assigned as part of a support team. 1975 was also the first year that referrals of suspected child abuse had been legally mandated, and it was our responsibility to see that this mandate was implemented in each of our assigned schools. It was Joan's first year as a school psychologist in Madison schools, though she had had considerable other experience. I had already served ten years, and this particular year, discouraged that an innovative service delivery model which six of us had piloted the previous year had not been approved for continuation, decided that I needed some additional challenge to help heal my disappointment.

So I had volunteered to include this particular school in my assignment, knowing that it would be a considerable challenge. It certainly was. With newly mandated responsibility to report suspicion of child abuse, in a school where I had not yet had time to build rapport with the teachers, I was feeling professionally unsafe - to say the least. In retrospect I have realized that I started Protective Behaviours because I wasn't feeling safe. The first theme, 'We all have a right to feel safe all the time,' was a message I needed to hear also.

The building Principal was a very 'nice' man who did not like to have his school seen as having problems, and reportedly could not be counted on to back up the of the higher-ups, but felt they had been unsuccessful in gaining support or additional resources. Discouraged, several of the teachers had requested and obtained transfer out of the school, and had been replaced by teachers new to the district, several relatively inexperienced.

The area this school served was indeed a unique one. At that time, it had the highest mobility of students in any Madison school, there were several low income housing complexes, but as yet there was little neighbourhood formation. There was a high percentage of families on welfare, and households in which adults, women particularly, worked outside the home in jobs that extended beyond the hours children were in school. There were numerous single parent households, unemployed people and people newly arrived in Madison, with very little adequate child care before or after school hours. There were frequently unemployed adult men present visiting or just hanging out drinking beer and watching TV. There were few parks or recreational facilities in the area. The family income was relatively lower and housing was shared and crowded. Often children were on their own a lot, went home to essentially unsupervised situations, or with slightly older children expected to be responsible for watching younger ones.

The area was culturally and racially diverse and becoming more so. There was considerable tension between the groups, adults and children. It was considered one of the least safe places in the city to live. A trend was beginning for people who could afford to, (mostly white families,) moving out. Several years later this school would be cited as not complying with educational racial integration, a situation that developed largely as a result of this housing pattern and which would result in exchange bussing students to alleviate the segregation. It was indeed a situation in which there were numerous barriers to doing the school-based support work in the ways we were then familiar with, although there certainly were untapped resources also.

Joan and I were concerned that our charge to learn about and report situations of suspected child abuse would be close to impossible unless we developed some access to information about the situations before they became of emergency crisis proportion. One of the teachers indicated to us that she would welcome some help, so one morning we arrived in her classroom to ask the children what they knew about safety and keeping themselves safe.

That's how it all started. A basic part of Protective Behaviours is about asking, not telling, and it's about feeling safe ourselves, as well as helping children keep safe.

For me, the preparation for that day in October 1975, had started many years earlier.

CHAPTER 1

EARLY DAYS AND NETWORK ROOTS

Looking back, I now realize I had an almost idyllic, very secure and protected childhood. I came home from the hospital to a newly built family home in which I lived until I left for college seventeen years later. I now know that money was a continual problem, but then as the youngest child, I was somewhat protected from this knowledge. My father often said, nostalgically, that I was one of the last of the 'prosperity babies' born in 1928, the year before the great depression of 1929. My father later lost his administrative job as a result of that depression's aftermath, and was under-employed thereafter for the rest of his life. Those were tight times. My mother must have been an incredible manager. I do recall coming upon her worriedly adding figures over the cheque book and frowning, but I don't recall feeling worried myself. She was a creative woman, very optimistic, and somehow succeeded in transforming much of the money crunch into a necessity for creativity, especially around holidays. These were the days before television, and by necessity and lack of money, we made much of our own fun, and were always encouraged to make presents. To this day I tend to value highly a present that someone makes for me!

I grew up on the lower edges of middle class. We had less money than our neighbours. My father's job was less secure, and exactly how much money he earned seemed like a secret. I had the impression that, in several of the tightest years, my mother's writing brought in more money than my father's five half day weekly job. He took the responsibility to be a provider very seriously and considered any money worries were his fault. As a youth, after his father's death, he had left high school to work to support his mother and frail younger brother. Although he later attended technical school, read extensively and was curious about the world, he seemed always to feel his lack of formal education strongly. He instilled college education expectations strongly in all of us - and it was later very satisfying to him that each of his three children not only finished college, but also earned graduate degrees.

In my early childhood, before the most serious of the money troubles, my father worked in an administrative job for an International Steel company, commuting an hour a day each way to New York City. He was a very gregarious person, and was always collecting interesting people and bringing them home for dinner, or for holiday celebrations. Largely due to his outgoing nature, we had contacts with people in many different countries and unusual professions. We rarely spent any holiday alone as a family. Usually there were house guests in our small home, and my sister and I doubled up in bed, or sometimes gave up our beds to camp on the floor.

For years later, letters, presents and cards would arrive from people who had spent time in our home. Neither of my parents had travelled much, nor did we have the means or expectations to travel extensively while I was growing up, but my parents both took many opportunities to bring the world into our home. So the assumption was probably reinforced by the strong advocacy of my sister on my behalf - both in the multi-age neighbourhood bunch that hung out together, and within my family as a go-between for me with my older brother and often even with my parents.

My mother, a former kindergarten teacher, enforced very firm rules about friendly play - and as most of the neighbourhood liked to gather in our yard - that too was a built-in protection. As the youngest in most of the groups I played with, and in the presence of my sister protector, I was encouraged and supported in lots of adventuring. Surprisingly, I remember few situations in which being the youngest seemed to be a disadvantage - I was rarely treated like a tag-a-long or a nuisance.

> *Later, in developing the Protective Behaviours Process, we defined an extended Network as at least four people, besides the people we live with, to whom we can turn if we're not feeling safe. These non-household adults, individually selected and checked out regarding their willingness and availability to listen and hear problems and successes, are in addition to the family or adults with whom we live. We learned from adult survivors and others the importance of non-household adults. While people with whom we live may be the first people many children turn to, if family members are not available, or are part of the problem, then we need trustworthy, available others. A Network, in Protective Behaviours terms, is at least four additional persons whom we feel we can trust to turn to if we feel unsafe, or (we later added) if we have something exciting to share. There are various kinds of Networks, for example, personal networks and those developed through sport or other interests, special purpose networks such as AA or ALANON, workplace networks, community networks and many more. For optimal protection, we learned that adults need to have more than one Network.*

While I was growing up, others in my immediate family maintained, explored and trusted many contacts with adults outside of our household. Looking back, it seems that I took the presence of networks for granted. Only later I learned about their vital importance for safety and adventure by experiencing their absence. I realized that it is sometimes necessary to consciously develop and maintain this vital support - it doesn't just happen for all children. It doesn't just happen for all adults.

....

My mother and father both loved the out-doors and encouraged my active participation in that world. For numerous years my father was responsible for maintaining a five mile section of the famous Appalachian Trail that runs along the east coast of the USA from Maine to Georgia. Often as a child, I accompanied him on long hikes and trail clearing treks, and one summer spent several weekends helping to build a trail shelter.

When we went walking my father had me make a practice of counting the small bright orange lizards that were numerous in those northern New Jersey woods.

'How many lizards so far?' he would ask me frequently as we hiked.

> Behaviours strategies. 'One Step Removed' is a strategy which provides a way to address situations that are potentially dangerous or frightening, allowing people to get information they need, without increasing fear and distrust. During those times with my father it was necessary for me to maintain my alertness. Surely this was a precursor of our Protective Behaviours claim that we can teach children how to protect themselves without scaring them to death. I knew already that there were copperheads and rattlesnakes in those woods, and I knew they were dangerous. Watching for orange lizards and sometimes feeding them encouraged me to enjoy the woods, to explore and adventure. Constant warnings to watch out for poisonous snakes would have constricted me and encouraged fearfulness.

....

The tall ladder was leaning against the house inviting the three year old Peg to a climbing adventure. My father, brother and sister were painting the house that summer, and the tall ladders were a constant presence. I stood at the bottom and looked far, far up at my eight year old sister busily painting. Tentatively, I reached out a hand and a foot to start up. Just then my father came around the corner of the house.

> 'Go on up, if you want,' my father encouraged, 'and when you get as high as you want to be, come on back down.'

I brought the other foot on to the first rung of the ladder.

> 'One thing to remember,' he added, 'you've got two hands and two feet. Four things to hold on with. Don't have two of them on the same rung at the same time. Hold on with three, move one.'

Sometime later, my sister showed me how that was useful in tree climbing, too. In the woods behind our house, in a small clearing in the blackberry brambles that we called the 'Pirates' Den' there was an ancient apple tree, obviously designed for climbing children. I remember my sister helping me start up into the broad inviting branches -

> 'One foot here, one foot here, now where is this hand going to go next?'

These were certainly encouraging adventurousness in the context of safety - and it worked well in my early childhood.

Then as I got older, as my world enlarged, and as I experimented further, I gradually found that my father's - and others' - feelings and boundaries about what was safe were often different from mine.

Sometimes, for instance, it was fun to balance quickly across a single branch no-handed, or to swing by my hands alone. One latter adventure cost me two stitches and a broken tooth when the branch broke, and strong reminders about the three hold ons after I had been sewn up. But it had been a glorious feeling before the branch broke - my ardor was not dimmed, I merely checked out the branches somewhat more carefully from then on. I hadn't developed the concept of Early Warning Signs or Early Alert Body Signs then, but I certainly had the experience.

> *Early Warning Signs, (EWS) as we define them in Protective Behaviours, are the first ways your body lets you know when you are not feeling safe, or that the risk is changing. These are adrenalin reactions. EWS are specific body sensations in specific body locations. They are internal, not visible to another person. Only I can tell when I have my EWS, and only I can tell when enough has happened and my EWS goes away. Some prefer the alternative phrase, Early Body Alert Signs. These signs are present in both dangerous and in adventurous situations.*
>
> *The concepts of Adventure and Safety are linked together in the Protective Behaviours Process. Our definition of safety includes adventurousness and risking. We all need some intensity in our lives. Boredom is not enlivening. Feeling safe is what we offer in Protective Behaviours, not being safe. Feeling safe in this context is always determined individually in response to internal criteria and involves risk taking. It is not a passive state of not climbing ladders or trees, of locked doors, staying off the streets after dark, or external reassurance. Protective Behaviours is about saying 'Yes!' to adventurous risking on purpose as strongly and effectively as saying 'No!' for protection.*

I also came to realize that, while my father consistently encouraged my physical adventurousness, what elicited my father's warning signs in other areas were often substantially different from what elicited mine. No blame, as the I Ching would say. I have since speculated on the whys of those differences - but the fact for me growing up was, they just were different. I spent quite some time untangling that - and some of his worries about money, and his fears about financial security are still tangled with mine to this day.

....

Six years old at the time, I can still recall the musty smell of the cellar as I sit at the top of the stairs with my dog, Roddy. We're sitting there together on a wintry afternoon, and it is rather cold and drafty. My nose is clogged up from my tears and I'm feeling very small and powerless. My beloved companion dog has committed some - now forgotten - misdemeanor and the grown-ups have temporarily banished her to the basement despite my most fervent protests. And what's more I had to put her here, so I feel that I've betrayed her. I'm feeling lonely, let-down with no one to tell or appeal to. I feel like the world is all against me. At six I didn't have much of a network outside of my family and this is one of the times I remember vividly the absence of someone to tell.

....

Another time of great loneliness and lack of perceived support I remember was a specific fall day, the first Saturday after my sister left home to go away to college. Bette and I had always spent much of our time together - she as a five year older sister had given me the gift of being her favorite person in the whole world, and I easily returned the feeling. She truly is a remarkable sister, and we were both daughters of a mother who knew the importance of sisters from her own two, and fostered a remarkable and wonderful closeness between us.

This morning I remember so clearly. I was eleven. I had retreated to the comfort of a special place of my childhood - the high branches of an oak tree which my father had transplanted from the mountain behind our house when I was born - 'Peggy's Tree.' I still remember the dry unique smell of the oak bark as I wrapped my arms around the trunk and wept, my tears darkening the light grey bark. A large piece of my network had collapsed, and at that moment I didn't realize that my sister too, was acutely homesick for me, and her college adventure was not all as brightly colored, engrossing and exciting as I was imagining for her. From that time on my social life was to change dramatically, and my peer network would become more central. But small Peg in the tree that day did not have the advantage of this hindsight. I felt utterly desolated and abandoned.

....

An excerpt from my mother's writings:[1]

Long ago in the dim days of childhood, someone pointed out to my skeptical mind that it was the minute grain of sand within the oyster's shell that caused the pearl to be produced: that this flawless gem developed as the direct result of an irritating, unwelcome element that had intruded into the otherwise peaceful and undisturbed life of the oyster ... Sand in the oyster! Surprising and unexpected values growing out of the difficulties and tragedies of life.

The pearl in the oyster was a metaphor that informed my mother's life and came to inform mine. The year before she died, on her ninetieth birthday, surrounded by ninety brilliant yellow daffodils, she presented each family member with a gift pearl.

> 'Pearls are what oysters do with the irritations of sand,' I remember her saying - and then with a twinkle. 'Have you made any pearls lately?'

> Or, ruefully, 'It's hard to see how this lumpy time is ever going to become a pearl!'

I have a special affinity for this metaphor, as my official, grown-up name, Margaret, means pearl.

---

[1] Florence M. Taylor *Sand in the Oyster,* unpublished manuscript

CHAPTER 2

OF MARRIAGE AND MOUNTAIN ADVENTURES

Adventures? Nasty disagreeable things! Make you late for dinner!

    Bilbo Baggins
    in response to Gandalf's invitation to go adventuring
    The Hobbit, J.R.R. Tolkien[2]

Yet regardless of this initial disparagement, Bilbo was not willing to miss sallying forth in answer to the invitation. And he was indeed late for numerous dinners - even missing some altogether!

There are different rules and expectations for adventures than there are for problems. For instance, I don't have to <u>solve</u> an adventure. All that is required of me is that I get through it. I don't necessarily expect to <u>like</u> all the parts of an adventure.

....

R, the man I was married to for twenty two years, was an adventurer physically as well as in science, and he aided and abetted this tendency in me. Together we shared many memorable expeditions and escapades. Frequently we took extended summer vacations on mountaineering trips to explore remote areas, mapping and climbing hitherto-unclimbed peaks, in the US and Canada. One summer, before our sons were born, we joined an expedition into the Chugach Range in Alaska. We flew in, landed on the glacier, served as human snow-shoed sled dogs and eventually climbed and named a whole range of snow covered peaks. One still unclimbed mountain, Mount Flandreau, was later named after me.

Somewhere I remember reading that we store in our memories moments not events. So it is with these many summers of mountaineering. Why is it, I wonder, that some of the many possible memory traces persist so vibrantly years later? In reviewing my own memorable moments, I've come to wonder whether the presence of Early Warning, or Body Alert Signs is one of the characteristics. In retrospect most, if not all, of the pieces recorded here do have that element.

---

[2] J.R.R. Tolkien *The Hobbit*. Allen and Unwin, London, 1978.

Virginia Wolff[3] in her writings suggests an older self as the future reader of her writings, especially of her diaries. Our Protective Behaviours concept of Inner Elder[4] grew from this idea - an older, wiser self who can be to us as adults, as we are to our own Kidselves.[5] I have been aided ever since by my own 'Old Peg', and more recently by a whole council of elders. Old Peg's encouragement has been crucial to me at numerous choice points of my life. One of her persistent ideas is that risking on purpose, living an adventurous life, is an excellent way to ensure a satisfying old age replete with stores of enriching memories. In writing this book, I have relished much of the revisiting. Here are three memories that persist.

....

June 1955 in the Chugach Range, Alaska. The wet snow continued, heavily, silently, piling up on our four small tents. I felt like I was hibernating, with only sporadic forays - when it was my turn - to dig out the tents to prevent their collapse over our heads, and to relieve a pressing bladder. It was my turn now, and looking around, chilled and snow-covered myself, I was very aware that we were four very small spots - the only spots - of human warmth on the surface of this remote Alaskan glacier. What happened to that hype about being able to see the sun at midnight in Alaska? We had been flown in four (or was it five?) days before, and had been snowshoeing across the Chugach glacier toward the mountains we wanted to climb when the weather allowed. Go for six hours, hole up for eight, then when the weather cleared, go for another four, hole up when it stormed. There had been lots of new snow since we arrived, and because it was light most of the time in between, we had lost track of conventional days. And now, since the last stop, it had been blowing a blizzard for the past ten hours.

The remoteness was awesome, suddenly I felt very alone and the desolate, frigid surroundings seemed foreboding. What was I doing here? Stamping and shaking some of the snow off, disheartened, I crawled back into protective shelter of my tent. This was a vacation?! I took off my soaked parka, changed into relatively dry socks and burrowed, shivering, into our damp sleeping bag. R. handed me a cup of tepid tea. I snuggled up to him and as my feet and hands slowly warmed, my mood changed abruptly. The tent seemed cozy. It was an epic adventure again and I felt safe. Safe? In the middle of a glacier in a blizzard? Yes. I felt safe.

....

---

[3] Wolff Virginia *A Writer's Diary*. Hogarth Press, London, 1953.

[4] see Chapter 6 for more comments by Old Peg.

[5] The Kidself is the child part alive within each of us. This is the part that is outrageously honest, intuitive, playful, loving, perceptive, creative, silly, profoundly serious, empathetic and curious. The concept differs from the Transactional Analysis concept of Inner Child in that the PB Kidself does not include the negatively socialised aspects that TA labels 'adapted child' and 'parent-in-child'.

August 1953, Teton Range, Wyoming, USA. Both skilled rock-climbers, we were alternating leads, moving one at a time, on the rock face of Mount Teewinot. We'd each already led several one hundred foot rope lengths, and were well up on the face. We were about to negotiate the most exposed part as I came level with R. who was taking in the rope which we both had tied around our waists. He had clipped a karabiner into a well-set piton,[6] and was protecting me in a standing belay on a narrow ledge, not wide enough to sit down on. There was barely room for his two feet and only one of mine, so I paused only briefly as he readjusted his hold on our climbing rope. Changing at that point from second to leader, I climbed past him to reach the exposed overhanging stretch beyond.

The first part of a lead beyond a belay spot is always the most precarious. The leader is no longer protected by a rope from above - indeed as leader I was taking the rope up to provide that protection from above to the climbers who would follow. Until I was able to place a piton and clip the rope into a karabiner, I was in double jeopardy. If I fell I would fall twice the distance that I had led before the rope would be of any use in slowing or stopping my fall.

'Ready?' I asked R.

'On belay' he rejoined. `See if you can find a lunch spot where we can sit down.'

I studied the steep lead ahead. No such ledges in sight.

'Maybe a sofa, too? I'll see what I can do!'

And I started up. It was the superb climbing rock that the Teton range is made of. The granite is nubbly enough to provide solid holds, but on this stretch, few cracks in which to position pitons. The rock warm under my hands, I was feeling exhilarated, balanced and glad to be back in the mountains. I moved lightly, yet carefully and was surprised to hear R. shout that I was half-way out. More than time to place a piton - yet there was no likely looking spot in sight. I moved sideways to see if there were other options. No luck, so I continued and just then came to a very tricky spot. Still no place for a piton. I was on it before I realized, and continued as that seemed safer than stopping. Seeking for the piton crack, I looked down and momentarily froze against the rock.

---

[6] A piton is a small metal climbing aid, rather like an inch-wide stubby flat needle, with an enlarged eye which can be hammered into a crack in the rock. When the piton is securely placed, a metal ring - the - karabiner - can be attached to the piton. The climbing rope is clipped through the karabiner behind the second person and tied. When arranged properly, the piton and karabiner provide protection for the stationary belayer, the person feeding out the rope. The theory is that the belayer, thus attached to the cliff face, can usuallly hold the fall of the climber without being pulled off the cliff face herself. Most times it does work!

This was my first climb of the season, and I was not yet used to the exposure - a process that I have to go through every year. It was a long way down, and suddenly the holds seemed to shrink and become less substantial. By now I realized I was seriously extended, verging on dangerous climbing, and still no piton spot materialized. Against much resistance, I willed my legs to move on. Two more moves on up. At last! A crack! Not only a crack, but a crack that had obviously been used before. Gratefully I eased my hammer around, selected the right piton from the jangle at my waist, and after a few ringing strokes of the hammer, clipped my rope into the very welcome karabiner. I shouted this information back to R. whose voice carried a sense of relief also. For a fleeting moment, I had a rope from above again.

Recently, I came across an exact rendering of this moment in climbing. Freya Stark,[7] traveller, author and adventurer describes her moment in the Italian Dolomites in the early 1900s, when she roped up for a difficult stretch on Le Petit Pousset:

> '...the happiness was almost frightening ... for the first time, I climbed with a rope ... the extraordinary sensation of safety, the abyss held in check, the valley with its life of everyday, bridges, tracks, fields and houses, seen from a narrow ledge which made it exciting and remote: this sense of double life is, I think, one of the main ingredients of the mountain sorcery.'

Sharing a similar moment, part way round the world and half a century later, I too looked down at the valley far beneath me, feeling the two realities at once. Taking a deep breath, I started off again in quest of that comfortable lunch spot. (Actually, as I recall, it was several leads further on - a small, but adequate ledge. No sofa, though!)

....

The third incident happened in July 1960, when my first-born son, Dave, was four years old, in the Selkirk Range, British Columbia, Canada.

> 'Come on up, Dave,' invited George, the wrangler who was herding the string of eight horses down the narrow little-used trail.

George was a taciturn mountain man who had lived near these mountains all his life and knew them well. He had helped us establish base camps in several areas of the British Columbia interior ranges on previous adult expeditions and we had come to trust and rely on his experience and advice. This expedition was different as our son was with us. Although Dave was an experienced camper by this time, this was the most extended trip we had taken him on. It was the second day of packing in. We were all wet, tired and eager to arrive at a good place for base camp so we could get settled in before the looming clouds poured rain on us - again. The horses were carrying the gear, the two wranglers were riding, and the rest of us were walking mostly, sometimes taking a turn on one of the extra horses.

---

[7] Stark Freya *Selected Travel Writings*, The Ecco Press. New York 1988.

A whole new side of George had emerged on this trip. He treasured kids, and delighted in them. He had Dave up on his horse with him most of the time, and had great stories to tell, things to show Dave, and eating treats from his saddle bags. So there was a whole unexpected facet to the trip. None of the rest of us had ever heard him talk so much before, and Dave had repeated much 'George-lore' to us the previous evening.

So four year old Dave clambered eagerly up behind George. A half mile further on, the trail disappeared into the river.

'Well,' I thought hopefully, 'we're pretty close, perhaps we can camp here.'

The river was higher than usual from several previous days of sunny weather that had produced an increased amount of glacier melt. The surging silt-laden water was hurrying away from its glacier-source as if it was being chased. The younger wrangler, Dennis, in the lead, had stopped the pack horses at the bank. But not George! He paused only long enough to shift young Dave around so he was sitting on the saddle in front of George (instead of behind), then handing one end of his saddle rope to Dennis, he rode right on into the rapidly moving water, trailing the rope that was to serve as a safety line for the rest of us crossing.

It all happened very fast, and when I realized what was up, George and Dave were well out into the river. I held my breath, my past trust in George's judgement eroding rapidly as the swiftly swirling water reached above stirrup level and George pulled his legs high. Just then the horse turned slightly upstream, and I caught a glimpse of Dave's face. To my surprise, his eyes were bright, sparkling, and he was grinning from ear to ear, laughing at George's exaggerated attempts to keep his feet dry. His trust in his new friend George was intact, and they were both fully enjoying this adventure. It was my hands that were suddenly cramped from holding on so tightly!

....

CHAPTER 3

MORE NETWORK LESSONS

Earlier, seven years married and having completed graduate school, I had moved to Madison Wisconsin where R. had accepted a faculty position. Our first son was born, big and healthy, but then developed some serious health problems. R., a university scientist, found some attractive, challenging and very lucrative opportunities for consulting work requiring that he travel out of town with increasing frequency - often for a week or more at a time. I found this difficult as a young mother as I was also attempting to continue professional interests and a part time job. Not only did I miss R. and his companionship, but the bulk of child care arrangements and the mechanics of household maintenance then devolved upon my less than willing shoulders.

Social life in a world of university faculty couples was also complicated by R.'s frequent absences. This was in 1957 when R. joined the Chemistry Department, and I was somewhat of an oddity as a wife who wanted a professional life of her own, worked outside the home, and maintained an active social life that was not composed primarily of other faculty wives. Although I was accepted, I never felt that I really 'fitted in.'

For instance, sometimes an invitation to a dinner party would come from another faculty wife for a time when R. would be out of town. It usually sounded like this:

> 'Hello Peg, (or often "Mrs West"). This is L.'s wife, June. We're having a dinner party a week from Saturday and would like you and R. to come if you're free.'

Early on I would answer,

> 'Well, that sounds like fun. R. will be out of town, but I'm free and would be happy to come.'

And not infrequently there would be an ... **awkward** ... silence. Sometimes the invitation would be postponed ... **awkwardly** ... although at least once I did attend a couples dinner party as the only non-attached (sort of) woman and found the constant solicitations of the host and hostess regarding my ease and comfort ... **awkward**.

I catch on quickly. I learned fast ... and my response came to be:

> 'Oh, too bad. R. will be out of town that night...' and I would pause, leaving a silence before, rather than after a possible acceptance.

Almost invariably the response would be,

> 'My, he travels a lot doesn't he? Well, we'll try again to catch you when he's in town.'

Partly as a result of these experiences, I developed some awareness about the oppression of enmeshment - which I came to call 'coupleism.' [8] Being one of a couple, which most of us are at some time or another, is different from coupleism. Two people can be in a couple relationship without engaging in enmeshment or coupleism, but it takes a high level of awareness and constant vigilance. The definition of coupleism which I came up with later is when two people act as one person vis-a-vis others. With R., I attempted to put this awareness into practice to the extent that I understood it then - for instance, as individuals, R. and I did maintain considerable autonomy with regard to friendships, and did invite people singly as individuals, not as couples, to our parties. We were careful not to speak for each other, using 'we' and 'us' sparingly and with circumspection. In practical time planning however, the reality was that R. was my primary relationship, others considered us coupled (and we were), and usually invited us together to social events. This meant that usually when R. was in town, he and I would assume access to each other, ie. time together on weekends, late evenings, early mornings, etc.

Besides the common example of speaking for each other, using plural pronouns (we, us,) I have since noticed several other aspects of coupleism. While people who are not in marriage-type relationships sometimes practice exclusion which could also be considered coupleism, this is more often named as such and commented on:

> 'Hey, that's two against one!'

> Or, 'You two are ganging up on me.'

One of the other things I've noticed is that two people in a coupleist relationship frequently physically or visually link themselves together by holding on to each other while talking to others, and by wearing matching or related clothing. Assuming access to each other, ie. assuming that interrupting or joining the other person at any time will be welcomed, is another marker. Within the couple, time apart is negotiated for, and time together assumed. There is an unwritten agreement that holidays and celebrations will be spent in each other's company. In the presence of others there are numerous private, inside jokes and innuendos that are not always clarified for others. Coupleism is often quite subtle, but that does not render it less oppressive. Our society and media today deftly reinforce and reward the practice of coupleism. Usually it is no longer as blatant as the dinner party examples given earlier, but it is ubiquitous none the less.

....

The years of my sons' childhood, (Dave was born in 1957 and A. in 1961), contained much learning about networks. I found it easier in many ways to form networks around needs of children. There are so many of us who are involved with children, and these are easy and available connections. I was still very much into being a super mom, working faculty wife with all the trimmings - suburban house, two cars, entertainment of foreign scientists, attractive children, slightly unusual clothes, adventurous summer vacations of mountaineering and winter skiing holidays.

---

[8] In reading this book in manuscript Sandy Litt commented that he feels this describes the first twelve months of a relationship, and some people never grow out of this stage.

I know now that I didn't know a lot about brothers - my own brother is eleven years older and wasn't around a lot when I was small. If I had it to do over, I'd develop a better network of support for helping brothers be brothers. I know about sisters, but somehow allowed myself to be convinced that it had to be different for brothers. R. had one younger brother, and his sibling experience was very different from mine. He and his brother were and are very different and R.'s experience with having a brother did not give him the kind of expectations I had for the mutual support and trust that my sister and I had. I wish my sons would have for themselves the ever available love and support from one another that Bette and I have had almost continually throughout our lives. There is still time, perhaps they yet will. And there is some comfort in my belief that our children choose us as parents just as we choose them as children.

While reviewing the above with Sue Gordon in manuscript form, she noted my assumption of parent responsibility for helping siblings be friends. She raised several questions. Do siblings also choose each other? Why do they need to be close just because they're brothers? Aren't they also free to choose their own network people?

On reflection I realized I'd answer yes to all the above. For years I've been carrying around some now released guilt and uneasiness because I'd bought into that unexamined assumption. Thank you, Sue.

....

One of the benefits of being married to an international scientist was travel. During the childhood years of my sons, I had the opportunity to learn how to build networks from scratch in two foreign countries - Japan and Germany, where we lived for a semester each.

In Japan, where I had some fluency with the language, I moved with relative ease into a neighbourhood as well as a professional network both of which were very enlivening for me.

One of my favorite memories is taking my three-year old son with a group of neighbourhood women and children to spend the day at the Depato in downtown Kyoto.

There's nothing like a Japanese Depato anywhere else in the world. It is ostensibly a department store, but yet much more. You start at the roof, where your children are immediately lured away by an inticing playground and playful, skilled child care workers. Then unhurriedly and deliciously you wend your way down through the floors of displays, art exhibits, flower arrangement competitions, food samples, fashion shows, new gadgets, cosmetics to experiment with, clothes to try on for fun or for buying, and it doesn't seem to matter to the sales staff whether you are playing or buying! Through a maze of descending escalators, gravity takes you inevitably to the basement where there is a gigantic supermarket where you can buy food for supper. Then back to the roof garden with other mothers to reclaim your children for the streetcar trip home, chattering now as a crowd of friends not just neighbours. I loved that time in Japan.

After being included in a couple of those playful Depato days, I was accepted in the neighbourhood, and had an available network for advice on any possible thing. This encouraged me to experiment especially with buying unfamiliar food at the local market - food which I often had no idea how to prepare. After purchases, I had only to walk out on to the dirt street in front of my house for a few minutes, encounter a neighbour or two, and enquire, 'Doo shimasho?' (What shall I do?) And they would gather round, examine my purchase and follow me into my kitchen or pull me into one of their homes, and soon, several cups of tea later, something luscious would have emerged. After a while they would invite me to go marketing with them, and would help me select unusual things. I certainly had an advanced and often hilarious course in Japanese cooking with the help of this spontaneous neighbourhood network - and I enhanced an already adventurous attitude toward cooking and eating which has enriched my life ever since.

It wasn't all smooth and easy, however. There were numerous times when only my sense of humour saved me.

One day, during this stay in Japan, I was on my way home after a meeting with a group of Japanese social workers when I became confused about which densha (streetcar) to take to my home on the outskirts of Kyoto.

I knew a moderate amount of Japanese by that time, and made a practice of speaking Japanese whenever I could. So on this occasion, I carefully composed a sentence in Japanese, asking the directions I needed. I practiced mentally, and then approached a young woman also waiting at the Densha stop.

> 'Ano ne...' I began, and then continued in Japanese, ' Does the densha for Takano Gawa stop here?'

She looked up startled, stared at my American face for a moment, uncomprehendingly. Then she shook her head apologetically, and answered slowly,

> 'Sorry. Not understanding English.' Her densha arrived and she hurried aboard.

I stood there nonplussed for a moment - reminding myself that I had spoken in Japanese, not English, and then started chuckling. I was joined in my laughter by another woman passing by who had witnessed the bi-lingual confusion. She came over to me and spoke rapidly in Japanese. Apparently my original query must have sounded good, because she didn't even bother to speak slowly. Smiling she walked on.

The only problem now was that, laughing and flustered as I was, I hadn't understood any of what she told me!

......

In Germany, however, where I lived for six months in 1968, and where I was addressed as 'Frau Herr Professor West,' I felt collapsed back into the role of accompanying wife. It felt very constricting. Lacking fluency with the German language, and living in the midst of downtown Wurtsburg, instead of a semi rural suburb as in Japan, I did not develop a spontaneous neighbourhood network. Nor was a professional network available, also partly due to my lack of fluency in German. Several faculty wives dutifully provided some social invitations, but my limited German made these difficult for me and them. I studied German laboriously, resenting the time and effort it took.

Because the boys were older now, six and eleven, I did not consider it necessary to arrange for additional child care coverage for the times they were not in school.

That also was a mistake, for then as it turned out neither they nor I had sufficient networks to keep us supported and interested in adventuring. At home in the US they were not accustomed to spending long hours together at home. Each had school all day, and various friends and activities. Here school only lasted until one pm and they were together in a small apartment on the tenth floor of the university gasthaus or occasionally in a nearby park to which an adult had to accompany them - me, usually. And it was fall, and often rainy in the afternoons. Cooped up together in the small apartment, the situation invited them to mischief. Punching all the stops of the elevator so that it stopped on every floor was a favorite. Dropping pumpkins and other splattable objects off the tenth story balcony onto the pristine entry terrace was another. Flying paper airplanes onto the immaculate sportsfield which backed onto the gasthaus building was another. We were not ideal tenants. Things got very tense. I got increasingly deenergized with severe chronic sinus infections. It was also during that time that I developed the first malignant skin lesion - skin cancer that was to haunt me, and eat away at my face for many years. I remember this as a lonely time. Although there were certainly some good times while we were in Wurzburg, the lack of supportive networks was serious for me.

Now, in retrospect I recognize - having seen the pattern at other times in my life over the ensuing years - that an insufficient support network was a contributing factor to the poor health I experienced during my time in Germany.

....

During these years, mid 1960s and early 70s, while I was coping, rather ungraciously at times, with R.'s frequent absences, I was also dealing with the major child care responsibilities for two growing children both of whom had serious health problems during their early years. As I was also experiencing invisibility as half a couple in the University community, I was slowly but surely enlarging my network and developing a more radical alternative social network which I moved into when R. was out of town. I developed woman friends through my work, and through them, met their friends, with whom I spent considerable time. Sometimes this worked out especially well, as in the case of one woman, (who didn't like R. much), with whom I had a long term friendship. I spent time with her when R. was on one of his frequent consulting trips. These networks overlapped a little with my traditional one which R. shared, but not much - they did not mix easily. Although having another network worked out relatively well for me for quite a while, eventually it became less than comfortable as the alternative network took on increasing attractiveness and invitations would come to me at times R. was in town that could not easily include him.

CHAPTER 4

BRACHIATING

Being on an airplane has always been special for me. It is a uniquely enclosed, rather timeless space, and on numerous occasions it has been a time when muddled or complex things become clear to me. One time I especially remember was in the late 1970's when I was in the midst of a turmoil about my life. My sons were relatively grown, and I had taken up the momentum of my own life, professionally and personally. Like many women my age in the seventies, the women's movement had opened new ideas for me, and new doors also. Professionally, as a school social worker, I was developing some of my own ideas, and felt there were lots of possibilities as I was able to devote more of my time and energy to my work. But my personal life was somewhat snarled up. As a result of some of the new opportunities and freedom from twenty four hour care of children, I found myself in the position of being in love with two men. It now seemed that I must decide which one of them I wanted to be with on a continuing basis. I was returning from an extended visit in California with one, en route now to the other. Decidedly I was smack in the middle of a transitional, rapidly changing time that many other women were also experiencing during those years. I had been grappling with this dilemma for several months, and seemed no closer to a solution. I wanted it all, and there seemed to be no way. So I was supposed to choose. And I didn't want to. Two future scenarios, both possible, but neither seemed whole and complete.

Suddenly it occured to me that maybe - just maybe - there might be another way. Instantaneously, another possibility presented itself.

'Oh!' I said, out loud.

The flight attendant was just passing by. He stopped and looked at me inquiringly. I shook my head, impatient to be back to my thoughts.

The idea-spark that had suddenly flared into my consciousness was - I could just be not-married. I didn't have to be married at all - not to anyone. I could just be single. I almost laughed out loud.

It may seem somewhat naive to some readers that it took me so long to realize the third option. I think one reason that prevented my seeing it was that I wasn't dissatisfied with my marriage in any major way. It had been a good, loving relationship, and it had not occurred to me that anything else could be better. It was not so much a pushing away of my marriage, or another marriage-type relationship, but a moving toward something else. What that something else was going to be was not yet clear, but the direction was.

A year later I had taken that risk. I left my marriage of twenty three years - much to the surprise of numerous friends and family. During that time, I continued to have a feeling of some surprise about the enduring confidence I had in my decision. Looking back, I realize it didn't have much to do with either of the men. Actually, I didn't have a lot of reasons for <u>not</u> wanting to be in a marriage relationship. It didn't make logical sense. I even had a hard time explaining it to myself. It seemed a large risk. What sustained me through my recurring puzzlement, and the surprise and judgements of others was that there was no persisting doubt in my mind after that sudden spark on the airplane. This was what I had to do now. So I did. In 1975, I became single.

During this time, several of us were doing some work in the schools to raise awareness about the effects of family change on children - divorce, separation, illness, death of a relative, death of a pet, unemployment, people leaving or moving in, etc. I wrote this poem about language use after one of our Family Change Task Force Meetings.

Some Thoughts on Family Change Terminology

nuclear families............and dispersed, inessential,
or uncentered families?

real mothers......and fake, artificial, unnatural,
intangible or unreal mothers?

broken homes....and whole, intact, perfect,
complete or unbroken homes?

average families...and deviant, abnormal, divergent,
incongruous or off-key families?

normal families......and irregular, disfunctional,
exceptional, erratic,
fitful, uncertain, variable,
capricious, disordered,
unsymmetrical, haphazard,
accidental, casual, chaotic,
hit or miss, uncontrolled,
unplanned, rough,
jagged, bouncy,
bumpy, craggy,
jolting, rugged,
scraggy, random - abnormal families?
traditional families....and unusual, rare, unique, diverse, alternative
or extraordinary families?

Journal excerpt (after a Family Change Task
Force Meeting Madison, Wisconsin October 1976)

In early September 1975, I was meditating in sun-speckled shade under the ash tree, with the verdant green of a bountifully moist late summer. I remember I was wearing a muted blue skirt with a subtle pattern that always reminded me of light on water. It was late afternoon, just before my sons were due home from school, a quiet interlude of welcome solitude when I felt well blended into the beautiful natural surroundings. It was a particularly welcome time as I was immersed in a difficult life transition - I had recently decided to leave my marriage. In preparation for that step, I had decided, among other things, to learn how to meditate, and to establish meditating regularly as a consistent practice. I had some instruction to get started and had found it easy and comforting. The incident described here happened about six weeks after I had started meditating.

Sitting quietly in the warm sun, I quieted my mind, noticing that both the cats had come to join me. Animals often like to join meditating humans it seems. The day had been hectic, and I had cleared this time with some difficulty from the midst of an overly busy schedule. I dropped easily and gratefully into the meditation place with my mantra and relaxed even more. After the usual subtle self-interruptions and distractions, I settled into a consistent quietness, and returned about twenty minutes of elapsed time later, relaxed and re-energized.

Before I opened my eyes, as I was returning my awareness fully to the immediate surroundings, I became conscious of a weight on my lap. It first crossed my mind that one of the cats had crawled up - but it was too light. As I opened my eyes, I looked, startled, into the dark, alert eyes ... of a small white bird, sitting quietly on my lap watching me! In the same instant of seeing the bird, apparently so vulnerable on my lap, I also became aware of my two cats, expert hunters, who were also still dozing beside me, one on each side. Neither of them had apparently noticed the bird, and I leaped into action. Scooping up a cat in each arm, I rose quickly, and deposited them on the other side of the nearby screen door. Turning back, somewhat perplexed, I noticed the bird still sitting quietly on the arm of my chair. I went back and sat down. She did not move, but sat there looking at me. I don't know how long we sat there, the bird and I, but I do know that a feeling of relief washed over me - relief and encouragement, a feeling of rightness. I sunk again meditatively into this feeling of peace, and when I returned to the ringing of the phone, the bird had gone. The cats, both annoyed at having been confined behind the door, came rushing out as I went in. In hunter mode, they both raced over to sniff inquisitively at the chair where the bird and I had been sitting. That memory of the white bird's visit will stay with me always - a special gift.

My mother, a deeply religious woman, took great comfort out of the bird's visit to me. To her it was a manifestation of the Holy Spirit who was reassuring <u>her</u> that all was well with me, and that she could trust that the separation and impending divorce was not the disaster that she had until then considered it.

The comment of the 'meditation checker' at the mediation center was a bit ho-hum:

> 'Oh! <u>Another</u> bird experience.'

The man who had been my marriage partner, commented only that he hadn't realized that people were keeping tame pigeons in the neighbourhood. Another friend interpreted it in terms of his beliefs - that it was a partial message from the world and that I should persist and <u>demand</u> from the bird spirit what the rest of the message was.

'But it wasn't a bird <u>spirit</u>, I felt the weight of her body on my lap ...'

None of the interpretations fitted the specialness of my experience - and I remember being a bit annoyed that others had decided what 'my' bird meant! Eventually, I realized it didn't matter. I came to let them have their interpretations freely and kept mine as a wordless experience of encouragement and affirmation.

....

A metaphor that sustained me during this transitional time was that of 'brachiating'. In my reading and study of non-human primates, I had learned of this phenomenon. Gibbons do it. Vervet monkeys do it, and so do numerous others of the long-bodied primates. Kids do it on playgrounds sometimes. When someone is brachiating they are swinging along by their arms alone, and they get going so fast that they let go with the back arm before they get a hold with the front arm. A moment of free flight in the midst of travelling.

That's how I felt sometimes then. I knew what I had let go of, but I was not yet sure what the next support would be. Sometimes it felt very adventurous, and sometimes it was more frightening than I wanted. Radical trust was necessary. It was good life practice, for I needed and used that skill of brachiating - and radical trust - many times in the ensuing years.

....

When I did leave my marriage in 1976, I was naively surprised and hurt that the network of faculty couples, where I had spent so much social time and energy, dissolved as support for me. The alternative network that I had been developing became a lifesaver.

It seems strange now, in 1990, looking back into the social mores of the seventies, to remember how painful and awkward I felt being who I was. In the seventies when I essentially left that faculty community by leaving my marriage, none of the chemistry faculty coupledom seemed comfortable in being friends with both R. and me, and none reached out to me during that time. It was a rude awakening in some ways. I thought I had a network, but it wasn't really mine - it had belonged primarily to my husband R.!

By this time however, I had learned well the necessity of multiple networks, and unconsciously had planned for a difficult time of transition. I was never again to be as devastated as I was that day in the oak tree after my sister left. Small Peg, my inner kidself, alive and healthy, hurting, yet safely protected inside of me, was grateful.

Shortly after the separation, my friend Donna came to stay with me briefly. She was recovering from some serious health and financial problems and needed a place to stay. Both of us were going through rocky times and I welcomed her presence and companionship.

At that particular time, as a mother I was feeling about one on a five point scale where five is high. As a wife, I felt I'd blown myself off the low end of the scale also. As a professional I could take a four and as a lover I was bouncing between two and five. As a friend I could often claim a four, but felt I was fading fast. Would I drain all my friends and be left with no support? I needed a lot of support right then. Donna and I both wisely realized that it was good that we both had other friends so that we could replenish ourselves separately. Strange and wondrous though, even when we were both down and discouraged and we'd curl up toe-to-toe on the living room sofa and talk, we'd both usually end up feeling much better. Two downs making an up? Two ups?

After one of these 'toe-to-toe' talks, as we came to call them, I observed,

>'I'm certainly lucky to have you for a friend.'

I was unprepared for Donna's explosive reply,

>'<u>Lucky!</u>' she stormed, 'There's nothing <u>lucky</u> about my being your friend!' She glared. 'I'm friends with you because you're the kind of friend you are. There's no <u>luck</u> about it.'

She softened and grinned at me.

>'Same to you,' I added slowly, taken aback.

>'No,' she persisted stubbornly. 'With me it's luck!'

We both burst out laughing.

....

Our Land Rover was kneeling up to her hub caps in a sand hole in the track we had been following all day. Stuck. I was sitting beside her, on the edge of the Dire Dawa desert, with a lukewarm, gritty serving of canned vienna sausage and bean sprouts in my lap. We were close to the end of our canned supplies. The blowing sand had permeated everywhere, and our jug of drinking water was warm enough to make tea even though it had been stored in the coolest part of the Land Rover all day. W. and I were sweaty and grumpy after two strenuous hours of trying to extricate our vehicle. We had decided to make camp for the night on the spot and hope for more success in the morning. It was indeed beautiful, but neither of us was doing very well at enjoying the surroundings or each other.

The foregoing incident occurred during the time that I had an opportunity to spend a summer in Ethiopia, as a Visiting Scholar at Haile Sellassie University in Addis Ababa, participating in a field study of Ethiopian baboons. Fortuitously, it also involved spending the time with W., a friend of long standing, whom I had known in graduate school and with whose family we had maintained contact over the years. He was in the process of leaving his marriage, as was I, and the summer was a pleasant, adventurous and passionate interlude for us both. Mostly. Ethiopia was his turf by that time - he had spent nearly a dozen years as Dean of Science at Haile Sellassie University, and was about to end that association and return to the States. His family had already left. And I knew no one else there. At first I wasn't much motivated to develop any relationships - it seemed unlikely that I would ever return to Ethiopia after that summer was over, and anyhow I was delighting in the days with W. So it was an almost unreal time out of time for me in many ways. The baboon observations themselves were absorbing, the travelling rugged, but entertaining and often breathtakingly beautiful. Our attempts to obtain the information and supplies we needed in remote villages where we had little language in common were challenging, to say the least. I've often thought that a training and practice in advance charades is probably the most useful thing a traveller to remote places can do in preparation.

It was only after three months, late in the summer, that this rigorous adventure of living as land rover nomads begin to wear thin, and my relationship with W. developed some gnarliness. Then I sorely missed the collective consultative wisdom of my Network people at home. Letters took two weeks round trip, so a dialogue was difficult to maintain, and spontaneous sorting out through any correspondence was too unwieldy. Phone conversations were expensive, unreliable and often had long pauses which resembled 'Earth to Mars' communication. I felt very extended, and quite lonely at times, particularly when things between W. and me were scraggy.

That summer I did learn some things about maintaining Networks long distance, and setting up ad hoc Networks quickly with new acquaintances. I added experience to my self-reliance and increased confidence in my ability to be snugly and contentedly alone - and to travel alone. These were all to stand me in good stead when later on I took other risks that meant that I would be alone for a while. A pearl grown from irritation again, but at the time in Ethiopia these just seemed to be bothersome lessons that I didn't want to learn.

Back to the stuck Land Rover, however. The next morning early, several families happened by. They were apparently on the way to market half a day's walk back the way we'd come. With great hilarity they surveyed the situation, pushed up and down on the bumpers - settling the Land Rover even more deeply into the ruts. Finally one of them, an older woman who had been thinking hard suddenly came up to us.

  'Proobleem?' she motioned toward the stuck Land Rover.

  'Yes, yes!' we nodded. 'Proobleem!'

'Ah!' she said, and turning spoke to the others who immediately put down their market goods, swarmed over the vehicle and soon extricated it. Laughter and cheers all around. We opened our last two cans of vienna sausage and passed them around. They headed back the way we had come, and we continued on to our next adventure.

....

Ethiopia

My culture-clad encounter
Makes little difference
To this ancient land -
Changing only me.

Addis Ababa

....

A disastrous example of a dissolving, changing network occurred when my eldest son was needing rehospitalization for a manic phase of his manic-depressive condition. He had not been accurately diagnosed at that time, and his craziness had started to get him in to occasional contact with law enforcement agencies as well as social service agencies. I had already experienced that his brushes with the law resulted in more rapid delivery of the services he needed - usually involuntary hospitalization - than did attempting to get him hospitalized through the more usual psychiatric channels.

At this particular time he was nineteen years old, and was acting very manic, was losing things, was picking up things, borrowing without permission - stealing - from several peer and family friends' homes where he had been crashing as a guest. Generally he was doing things that embarrassed middle class morality. I started receiving calls from people who were parents of his friends and known to me through school connections. They kept telling me that Dave was acting strangely and needed help. I kept telling them I knew this and suggesting that the best and kindest thing to do would be to inform the police so he could start getting the help he needed. Stalemate.

For several long weeks, these well-meaning but misguided people covered for Dave Middle class people do not report their friends' sons to the police. They don't want to embarrass anyone. So these otherwise sane people put up with burglary, unwanted raids on their refrigerators, general harassment - and called me. I was frantic. Finally, after numerous phone conversations, one parent to whom I am eternally grateful, did report, and help started.

Here a Network that had been useful and supportive for both Dave and me during D's high school years suddenly became ineffective when depended upon in a changing situation.

....

Upset after visiting Dave in the hospital psych unit, finding him still very manic and scarcely improved, I drove out of Madison to Gibraltar Rock Park.

There I climbed and sat high on an overhanging cliff, my legs dangling out over nothingness - drinking in the mind messages of danger ... but from a safe body position. I meditated in slow stages, alternating moments of closed eyes, with opening my eyes until the lurch of perceived danger of my physically exposed yet safe position, dwindled. Finally I could stay grounded with eyes closed or open - it was all the same ... and my inner reality held firm. This firmness rooted in me and still persists.

> Journal excerpt
> last day of August 1980

Further thoughts about the Gibraltar Rock meditation ... sometimes early warning signs of danger or warning persist by habit about a situation in the past - inviting me to obsess about situations I cannot change. In this example, past mothering of Dave Then it is necessary to impose another frame - to interrupt the old perceptions of guilt and blame - attitudes which are indeed dangerous and unproductive. Would this body metaphor work also to ease anxiety about present decisions to take risks?

Very powerful - a strategy to remember - nuts and bolts for externalizing internal stress. Useful in present crisis, or for interrupting obsessive self-blaming about the past. Impossible not to stay in the present!

> September 5, 1980

She Made Me Do It!

> Today on the bluff,
> Feet dangling
> The river ripples
> Duck calls, trees
> And the wind
> Mantra-ed at me
> Until my me-ness
> Loosened.

> November 10, 1983
> at Cactus Bluff
> remembering Gibraltar Rock

....

So I brought to the initiating of the Protective Behaviours Process a healthy respect for the necessity of Networks. Though I hadn't conceptualized the idea into words, I had been developing my basic awareness for longer than I realized.

I later summarized some of my thoughts about Networks.

'... having a Network can be like having insurance. I certainly don't expect to have all those things happen that I am insured against. What insurance provides is potential additional resources just in case. Often having some insurance can help you feel safe enough to take more risks, to have more adventures. It seems to me that this is true for relationships also. When I have a strong supportive Network, I'm more likely to provide myself with loving, healthy, adventurous relationships. It's when I'm feeling alone and unsupported that I'm more likely to settle for something less healthy, or even for victimizing interactions...' [9]

---

[9] West Peg Flandreau, *The Basic Essentials Essence Publications*. Adelaide 1989.

CHAPTER 5

NO MORE NIGHTMARES!

Scene in my Social Work Office, Midvale School 1974:

> 'I'm trying to get this done before our group meets,' I complained to Coyla, my office mate.
>
> 'Only *trying*?' commented Coyla.
>
> 'Yuk!' I said. 'That's a persistent one for me! OK - I'm <u>doing</u> part of this before group.'
>
> *In 1974, at Midvale School, School Psychologist Coyla Rankin and I had decided to look at what we called, initially, 'victim language.' We had agreed that we would call to attention usage that we noticed in each other's talking and writing. The impetus had come from a children's group that we were facilitating together in which we had noticed a lot of self-discounts and put-downs among the children. We were casting about for ideas to confront and raise the children's awareness of this destructive self talk, and in the process, of course, recognized that our own language included quite a bit also.*

Shortly after Coyla and I decided this, I was home one afternoon with our twelve year old foster child, who was out of school recovering from a cold. He was bored and somewhat grumpy, and I had an idea. I explained to him the contract Coyla and I had about language, and asked if he'd like to help me clean up my language until dinner time. An invited opportunity to be critical? He jumped at the chance so enthusiastically that I was a bit taken aback.

'And how about you pay me for ones that I notice?' he suggested.

Hmm, this was getting a bit more serious than I had intended. However, I decided to take the risk. It was only three hours, and I had already had some practice noticing. We made it mutual - he would also pay if he used any of the phrases we identified, or did self put-downs. Together we identified several phrases that I knew I used sometimes - try, work on, work at, attempt, hope, and the verb 'make' about people or feelings. We agreed on ten cents for most of them, but twenty five cents for the ones I identified as the three I most wanted to stop using. He was saving for a bike and I figured this was in a good cause, so I was willing to be generous. So I might lose a dollar or so.

This youngster had always been very articulate and a good conversationalist when he wanted to be. This afternoon it was in his own best interests to keep me conversationally involved. And he did. We had a great, wide ranging talk with few pauses. I was pleased also, as he had not been particularly talkative with me recently. His interest is this new project did not flag.

The afternoon was additionally productive for me, in that together we identified some new phrases that seemed to be in the same category - 'I don't know' (sometimes); 'just'; 'only'; 'really'; and 'I want you to want to ...(be with me.)' Also 'I'd like it if you would ...'; 'I don't suppose you would ...'; and 'You wouldn't like to, would you?' In fact, would, wouldn't, both seem suspect in some way that is not yet clear to us. Negative questions, too. Also, add-ons at the end of statements, eg. 'I'm going out now, all right?' or even, 'It's a cold day, y'know?' They all seem to whittle away at empowerment and credibility.

At the end of the afternoon I was startled to discover that I owed my young friend $10.75! Even after we deducted his considerably smaller score, he was more than $8.00 ahead. He was elated and I had certainly had an illuminating afternoon. I became irreversibly aware of the extent to which I infiltrated my language with the phrases we had already identified.

Later, as part of the Protective Behaviours Process, we came to use and suggest such contracts for various changes - regarding more language that does not invite empowerment, and also to interrupt language that was derived from military usage, and other violent phrases and metaphors or euphemisms that covered or disguised violence, eg. dressed fit to kill; target groups; rule of thumb. I have always found it easier, somehow, to notice something in another person, rather than in myself. So why not use this to my own benefit, I decided. And later yet, I realized that I could make contracts with myself to stop obsessive thoughts and catastrophising about the future, eg. regarding sufficiency of money, about my own abilities, and about relationships. Someone then told me that this is called 'thought stopping.' Whatever, I now find it useful and effective - an internal application of the strategy we call Protective Interrupting.

....

Here's an example of Protective Interrupting from a Domestic Violence Session:

Young Person: Last night at my house ...

Me: Wait a sec - right now we're talking about 'Suppose the people you live with are fighting ... or What if a friend told you ...

Young Person: Oh! But they were...

Me: Right now, for this discussion, I want you to pretend that a friend told you that. Afterwards, let's talk more about it, if you want. (To group as a whole) If this is happening in your home, or to someone you know, you don't have to settle for that. You can tell your Network people. Or you could tell me.

Me: (Writing on Brainstorm list) 'Tell someone.' Good. That's one of the first things you could do. Who could you tell? Let's review who those Network people could be.

After group, I sought this young person out and asked her if she wanted to talk some more about what was going on.

Incident at Franklin School
Madison, Wisconsin (USA) Winter 1978

*Note that in this example we consistently use **One Step Removed** language, ie. 'if this is happening ...'. We also avoid the **Command Mode**. We say 'You could tell someone', rather than 'You should tell someone right away.' Encouraging self empowerment is sometimes subtle. When we say 'could', the decision remains with the person involved, when we say 'should', we are using the **Command Mode** and telling the other person what to do.*

For people enmeshed in victimizing situations that they have not yet dared to talk with anyone about, the use of words like 'should', 'right away', 'always' can increase feelings of hopelessness. These words may invite feelings of guilt and self-blame for not having told sooner. 'You should' is often heard as judgmental. 'You could tell' holds out hope and increased options.

....

The plane had taken off uneventfully, and now dinner had arrived. Books were put away, and conversations started. A few exchanges with the man in the seat next to me had established him as a corporate executive and father. And now, in the temporary lull that had followed my brief answer to his question of what I do for a living, I could anticipate what was about to ensue. Then he started.

'You know, there was a situation like that back home where a young kid ...'

'Wait a sec,' I interjected quickly ...

The strategy of Protective Interrupting was initially developed as a way of stopping someone from self-disclosing in a context that would increase their victimization, as in the session example above. The idea has since been enlarged to include interrupting to prevent situations that are unwanted and presently or potentially victimizing to our kidselves.

On airplanes, at meetings, at parties and at other informal times, people often respond to hearing about my work with Protective Behaviours by preparing to tell me a secondhand, 'ain't it awful' horrible account of abuse. I used to listen sympathetically, and end up feeling drained and de-energized.

After working with Protective Behaviours for a while, I internalized the process still further. I decided that I was no longer willing to listen to horrible recounts unless they are in a context of problem solving and empowerment, with the teller willing to consider with me that the horror is stoppable. Those of us working against violence know it exists, already we know it is horrible, and we know there is a lot of it. We could exchange many examples endlessly and increase all of our feelings of discouragement and powerlessness. So now I Protectively Interrupt these disclosures to protect myself, and the teller, from reinforcement of victim thinking and the undermining of our energies - and to invite them into some active problem-solving.

'Hey, wait a sec ...' I interrupt, and then continue, 'Is this a situation you're still involved in? If so, I'm willing to problem solve possible interventions with them. And if not, I continue to suggest that there are people who do still need to be convinced that abuse like that is still happening, and that it is horrible, and that it needs to be stopped. But I'm not one of them. I already know more examples than I need to.

But there are people who need to know. People who don't know the horrors exist. So who are those people who still need to be convinced? And how can you get a detailed account to one of them?'

Then the conversation has a chance of continuing in a more productive way.

By Protectively Interrupting and redirecting in this way, I feel we can protect our own precious energies which we all need to get on with our work of empowerment.

....

On the way home today in the car after hiking at Parfrey's Glen, one of the women, C., was very tired. She volunteered that she hadn't been sleeping well at nights because of a recurrent nightmare.

I was reminded of some work I'd done about dreams.

> *'You don't have to settle for being scared in your dreams,' I ventured slowly. 'There are some other options we've been working on.'*

> *'Oh? What kind of options?'*

> *'Protective Interrupting, I bet' oechimed in another woman. 'But how does it work with dreams?'*

As the other women already knew something about Protective Behaviours, I did an 'instant PBs' about the first theme and Protective Interrupting, and helped C. identify one of her Early Body Alert Signs.

> *'So,' I finished up, 'before you go to sleep, make an agreement with yourself that you'll wake up when you feel your Body Alert Sign. Then use the first theme - We all have a right to feel safe - even when we're asleep - as an affirmation or mantra as you fall asleep.'*

"That's called "lucid dreaming" isn't it?" asked one of the other women.

'Yep,' I grinned, 'Lucid Dreaming 101 Mobile Lab Section.'

Two weeks later, C. called me.

'It works, Peg,' she started.

It took me a moment to track in on what she was talking about as she rushed on.

'I woke up twice just as the scary part was about to happen, then used the theme to get back to sleep. I use that every night now, and I haven't had the dream since! Is it always that easy? Why doesn't everyone know?'

Journal excerpt
April 1989

There were several stages to the development of the idea that we have a right to feel safe - even when asleep ... or perhaps especially when asleep. It is essentially an extension of the Protective Interruption Strategy and the use of the first theme as an affirmational statement to support self-empowerment.

The roots go way back to when my now adult children were small - long before we had put Protective Behaviours together as such. They had the inevitable nightmares. Dave spontaneously developed a bedtime ritual. He had earlier received a gift of a mounted blue morpho butterfly as a birthday gift, and, entranced, had spent long periods with the changing iridescent reflections of the wings. Each night after Dave was in bed he would take an imaginary trip through our home, opening doors, drawers, cabinets. At each opening, he would imagine that a flock of blue morpho butterflies flew out and circled gently around him. At first I shared the imagery he had developed by having him imagine it out loud, and then later he came to do it silently by himself. It worked for him. After a while whenever he came upon an adventure or scare in a dream, he would immediately imagine blue butterflies circling protectively around him - or wake up if he couldn't imagine them.

I didn't recognize until twenty years later that Dave and I were doing it the hard way - second step first. I later learned, from other children, that it's much easier to <u>first</u> teach someone to wake up to an Early Body Alert Sign, and <u>then,</u> as a second step, incorporate some empowering imagery and strategies.

During my years as a school social worker, I frequently talked with children who were experiencing recurrent nightmares. At one point I also came across the Senoi Method of Dream Analysis. I used the ideas myself and with a woman's therapy group I had going at the time. I soon realized that some of these ideas might be very effective in my work in developing Protective Behaviours and in helping the children prevent frightening dreams.

Reportedly this dream analysis method was used by the Senoi Islanders in Malaysia.[10] For them apparently, the dreaming and the waking were both considered equally important aspects of reality. In their view, one was responsible for actions in dreams as well as in waking. Each morning all would share their dreams and decide what actions were needed as a result. Children were given guidance by older people, and it was said that Senoi children never had nightmares, such as our children have, after they were old enough to describe their dreams and do their unfinished dream work in the waking state. Quite an intriguing idea, I thought.

There was very specific advice given to children depending on what emotion they were experiencing in the dream. For example, if the dream involved running away and fear was the primary emotion, then that pointed to the need for allies. One was instructed to stop running away, to call allies, and to turn and face the danger while the allies assembled. Additionally it was suggested that the dreamer directly ask the chaser what was wanted of the dreamer. Often, it was suggested that the chaser had an important gift for the dreamer that the dreamer needed to ask for and decide whether to accept. Similarly, falling dreams were reframed as precursors to flying dreams, or a situation in which a dream spirit was pulling the dreamer down in order to give a gift. Fear in a dream also meant the nearness of great power that would soon be available to the dreamer.

Often when a child had been frightened or confused in a dream, the adults would problem-solve with the expectation that the child could redream the dream to a more satisfactory outcome.

The Senoi further believed that dream reality was more easily influenced by the dreamer than was waking reality. For instance, they would suggest to young dreamers that small things could become large, and have unusual powers. Dreamers could fly in the dream world, could become large or small or invisible at will, as well as other wonderful things. Many increased options became available.

Deciding to explore using some of these ideas with young children, I did some quick surveys with six to nine year old children in school classrooms, and found that a majority of the children reported have recurring frightening nightmares. I found very soon that many of the Senoi ideas fit in extremely well with the developing PB concepts.

For the 'Dreams Project,' Nancy Marshall Moore and I enlarged the Protective Behaviours first theme as : 'We all have a right to feel safe ... even when asleep.' Then we planted the awareness that we can feel our Early Warning Signs even when we are asleep, and can use them as a cue to wake up when we decide to.

The children grasped this idea readily, with minimal explanation, and started using it to escape from frightening situations in their dreams.

---

[10] I've not yet been able to locate exactly where in Malaysia, or how accurate these roots are. Perhaps it doesn't matter as the ideas, wherever they originated, have considerable wisdom.

As a further step, after a child had learned to use the Early Warning Signs as a cue to wake up, we brainstormed some of the ways in which the dream reality might be different from waking reality. The children readily told us ideas that they had experienced in dreams - teddy bears had become large, protective and ferocious against a danger; a small flower growing out of the edge of a cliff had grown large enough to catch a falling dreamer; helicopters arrived when called to rescue someone from a burning building; many birds came suddenly and created such a disturbance and screening that the dreamer was easily able to slip away unseen; an earthquake happened and opened a large rift between the dreamer and the danger; a guide appeared who knew a way out, etc. Many of the children had already had such empowering dream experiences.

Following this discussion, we then had each child draw a scary dream they had dreamed. After they had finished, we asked them to turn the paper over, and using the ideas from the group brainstorm, or other ideas of their own, change the ending of the dream so that they felt safe again.

In a follow-up with more than fifty children, more than 84 per cent reported using Early Warning Signs as a wake-up cue, or other empowering ideas for modifying fear-inducing dreams.

But, you may wonder, as I did initially, isn't it dangerous psychologically, to interrupt dreams? Doesn't it interfere with psychic work we need to do? Might it not short circuit information we need?

Intuitively, I don't think so. And in our experience with the children and informally with others, and myself, there have not seemed to be any noticeable negative effects. We've probably all had enough experience in feeling scared and powerless - I doubt that any of us need <u>practice</u> these feelings anymore. In fact, quite the opposite, it seems to me, as I see one of the basic problems in our world today is that we are encouraged into denial and apathy, we are encouraged to 'numb out' feelings of fear and powerlessness in order to avoid the feelings of despair that situations of continuing fear and powerlessness generate. Thus a vicious cycle is set up that allows the continued development of dangerous military power, racism, classism, homophobia and ageism.

What the ideas described in this chapter apparently provide, in a metaphoric way, are ways to interrupt feeling scared or powerless and to work out solutions. My own experience, and reports from children and others bear this out. The increased feelings of personal power due to having some control over interrupting frightening dream situations apparently serve as practice for self empowerment in the dreams world certainly, and perhaps in the waking world as well. We need all the practice in self-empowerment that we can get. Who knows - maybe the Senoi are right. Maybe dream states and waking states together make up our reality and skill learned in one state are available in the other. Seems to work that way for me.

Here are some other examples of ways in which people of all ages have used the strategy of Protective Interrupting.

Ann Brickson's family including five year old Chris were at supper. Ann had just read a pre-print of this chapter and was sharing some of the ideas with her husband. Chris listened and then entered the conversation, saying he had bad dreams sometimes. So they talked about what he could do and one of the ideas was that his stuffed bear, 'Brown Bear', who was his sleeptime companion, might be able to help.

Two days later, in the early morning, Ann heard Chris stirring, and went in to check on him.

'It's OK, Mom,' said Chris sleepily, 'I just had a bad dream, but Brown Bear took care of it.' And he went peacefully back to sleep.

Next morning he excitedly shared that, in his dream, a bunch of men on motorcycles were chasing him, and throwing bombs. Brown Bear, big and strong, threw houses at them, and the motorcyclists got lost inside the houses. Chris, suddenly able to run faster than ever before, had got away easily.

'And he didn't seem scared - just sort of excited and proud of himself!' Ann added.

                                 - Madison, Wisconsin USA
                                 September 1990

....

Two-and-a-half-year-old Meg was riding on Joel's back. She was telling her father about a recurring scary dream.

'Are there any people nearby in the dream?' he wondered to her.

The conversation continued. After a while he suggested,

'You could have me come into your dream ...'

While Meg was considering that suggestion, her five year-old sister, Lia, mused out loud,

'Well...she might not have as many adventures that way ...'

                           - Tora Huntington, Lia and Meg's mother
                           8/27/90 Cape Cod, Massachusetts

....

Incidental to a consultation with me, a patient reported that her son's school had introduced the Protective Behaviours Program. As a result her eight year old son in time reported that he experienced his Early Warning Sign every Friday when his father came home. My patient said her husband was in the habit of drinking after work with his associates on a Friday. By the time he got home he was usually 'fairly chemical' and his sarcastic use of language 'bordered on verbal abuse.'

My patient relayed her anxiety to her husband and suggested she would take the children to McDonalds for tea every Friday if he would agree to be in bed by the time the family returned so as they could all 'feel safe.'

This option worked for a while, and in time the father was so shocked that his absence made his family feel safer that he joined Alcoholics Anonymous. He also acknowledges that it was the 'gentleness' of Protective Behaviours language that made him confront his problem.

                                    Reported by:
                                    Dr. Elizabeth F. MacMahon M.B., CHB.
                                    Victoria, Australia

---

[11] Editor's note. Maybe the next step is to talk to this father about Victim Language!

CHAPTER 6

POEMS AND JOURNAL EXCERPTS

There were many heart-wrenching child abuse situations I encountered during my thirteen years as a school social worker. The memories of this one persist.

A young boy, new to our school, was brought to my attention by his teacher on the child's birthday. The teacher had offered a birthday hug and the child winced in pain. He was severely bruised. This contact resulted in a disclosure, a referral, and it was found that the child and his family had been reported before, and already had an active file at the county social services.

Relationships between numerous School Social Workers and County Social Services Social Workers were somewhat strained at this time. Referrals had increased dramatically as a result of the Protective Behaviours implementations in some schools, and the County Social Workers' caseloads had reflected the increase. Many were overloaded, as were we. There was considerable dissatisfaction on both sides as to how priorities were set and how referrals were handled. Administrators from both agencies were in the midst of a long process working out an inter-agency agreement regarding referral procedure, and had made it clear that they didn't want the boat rocked.

Because the County already had an open file on this child's situation, there was some pressure not to pursue it further, but to assume, 'in good faith' that all was being done that could be done. But the child was still being beaten - scars and bruises at various stages of healing documented this. The Principal at this school, which was one of the first where Protective Behaviours became well established, was very supportive, and together we pursued the situation.

A court hearing was held at which I testified, and the child was temporarily removed from his home pending the establishment of a more protective network and linking to resources. It was a traumatic situation all around - and my own self-doubts surfaced numerous times. The child was 'protected' from further physical abuse, but the cost was high. I now have a vision of a legal system based on healing rather than blaming - but at that time I didn't. It was agonizing to see this family blamed and further victimized by the system - and by me as a part of it.

The three poems that follow were written during this time, and reflect some of my heartache.

Who are you, Peggy?

*I could have been her.
Her name was Peggy, too,
A worn-down, frightened woman
Trying not to cry in court.
I could have been her
Sleeping little, working nights
On a dull, boring job
Living with a noisy man
Who woke me up
When he was hungry.*

*I could have been her
Too little money
Too much hopeless anger
The world bouncing grey
Off my black skin.*

*I could have been her
Looking through dying dreams
Watching my son
Grow sassy and stubborn
Love scabbing over.*

*I could have been her
Tired of the endless fog
Awakened once too often
By those menfolks yelling.*

*I could have been her
Suddenly striking out
Surprising myself
Embodying my protest
At this world's injustice
By bruising my son's small body.*

*She could have been me
Testifying in court
About bruises.*

September 1981

The Cost Of Paying The Rent

It was his seventh birthday
His new teacher at his new school
Hugged him in a birthday hug.
He winced.

'Oh? You don't like hugs?'
The teacher asked, thoughtful.
'No!' he said 'Don't! It hurts!'
'Why does it hurt?' the teacher asked
'No!' the child looked trapped
'I can't tell. I'd get ...'
'Get what?'
'Another whupping ...'

Later I looked carefully
At his small bruised body
Scars and scabs showing
That this was not
A one-time beating.

She hit me with his belt
because I drank the milk.

She works at night
And has to sleep 'til four.
And she got woken up
And mad.

That Billy ...
He don't give her no rest
He wakes her up to cook
Whenever *he's* hungry.

He's got to stay
Because he pays the rent, you know
And I eat last, after *he's* done.

He yelled and hit me first
Because there was no milk.
That woke my mother up.

I ate the cereal and milk
So she could rest
And wouldn't have to cook.
I put some coffee out for Billy, too
But Billy wanted milk
And yelled and hit
And woke her up.
It used to be...
Sometimes she'd make him stop.
This time she hit me, too.

Don't tell her that I told you.
PLEASE!'

     September 1981
     Schenk School
     Madison, Wisconsin

'It Was Just A Whupping' - The Status Quo Talks Back

'It was just a whupping.'
You should have just written your report,
Referred to proper authorities
And let it go.
Why must you meddle on?
That would have been enough
To do your job, efficiently and well
And pass it on.

But no. You had to go to court
Feed on the drama
Attempt to fix the world
Take on the system... again.

Does it really matter?
If you had not made such a fuss,
The DA might have held his ground
Without you there, talking of scabs.

It was just a whupping
A little reddening, no scars, no scabs.
You must not see the scabs next time.

Next time don't look so close
Let the experts decide what's safe
That's what they're for.

You wanted to look good
So the Principal and teachers would say
'She gets things done.'
And now maybe
He'll never go home
And he may be abused
In that licensed foster home.

You've gotten unprofessional
Soft, emotional
And so judgmental
So sure you're right.

It was just a whupping.
You should have just
Written your report
And let it go.

October 1981

Journal Excerpts: October 1980 - June 1981

October 12/80.

During a long days drive today, to visit my sister in Ohio, I noticed a Railroad Crossing marked

EXEMPT

meaning that we don't have to pay any attention to it ... On reflection, it seems to me that we could use this concept other places in our lives. Imagine a rubber stamp for stamping

EXEMPT

on parking tickets, bank overdrafts, for use instead of a postage stamp if you're out, on a piece of paper for a potluck, contributions, requests for money of any kind that we approve of but can't afford, inter-office memos of various sorts, meeting notices, invitations, requests, surveys, questionnaires, forms, renewals ... the list seems endless.

December 12/80.

Had shared the above idea with Barbara. She called tonight to ask if I had got the EXEMPT stamp yet because she needed it immediately! Today she had a whole day she wants to EXEMPT!

June 12/81.

Arrived in the mail today - a small package from Barbara, now living in Arizona. It contained a rubber stamp for stamping

EXEMPT

No note - no comment ... just the rubber stamp.

In 1990, looking back on this exchange, I realise that it was a playful pre-cursor of Protective Interrupting! Maybe the incident which follows is another example.

Things have been very harried lately. Yesterday I told the world, 'I need more time for meditation.'

> *So today the world*
> *Gave me*
> *An hour and a half*
> *To wait*
> *and meditate*
> *at the gas station*
> *while my car was being fixed!*

Author's journal
March 5, 1983

....

Three hour Protective Behaviours, the first system-wide Protective Behaviours Training for Madison Schools.[12] *One representative from each elementary school. Several building administrators also attended. The three hour time slot shared by two other school social workers (not of my choosing). Again a familiar feeling that I was expected to oversimplify and sell the PB program, without sufficient time to do it justice. Just a quick run through without time for experientials that would help participants to ground and internalize the ideas. I was unprepared for the obvious resistance of some of the administrators, and felt my place in the staff hierarchy as well as time constraints made it impossible for us all to deal*

---

[12] This was before I realised that short sessions should be called briefings, reserving the term Trainings for sessions of four hours or more.

effectively with the resistance. The denying of children's reality ... unwillingness to call unwanted touching 'sexual abuse'. Discouraging. Not completely balanced by the many positive appreciative comments and written evaluations. This is the group I potentially can have the most influence with. (Or is it? If not here, where?)[13] So my expectations were perhaps unrealistic. And then a co-leader using victim language in the brainstorm role play modelling. Yuk! Is it unrealistic to expect people to internalize the Protective Behaviours ideas with short trainings? The ideas seem so simple, but resistance gets in the way. And my own use of victim language is still under my constant scrutiny - and contracts with others. Progress not perfection? Yet even this abbreviated watered down version of PB is too much for some of the administrators, several of whom left early.

October 5, 1982
Journal excerpt

Myers, a graduate student and abuse survivor, has volunteered to help me make a Protective Behaviours video tape. So that's what we did. This is new ground for me and it is more complicated than I had anticipated. I sometimes get discouraged. No funding available. So little time, and my energy feels very extended. Will we be able to pull this off - and will it make a difference?

One night, tired and small-visioned after an extended editing session, I wrote this poem.

*Bright TV lights
Affirm the effort
Prepared questions
Elicit thoughtful answers
And careful statistical comments*

*While beyond this film
These sordid statistics manifest
Shadowing trust and innocence
With their bruising reality*

*The floodlights fade
My face and voice rerun
As flickering light in a dark room.*

---

[13] Well as it turned out this wasn't the group that caught the larger vision of protective Behaviours. There were other places - many other places, but I didn't know that then. I wish I had!

A talking shadow self
To chase the shadows?
It seems so flimsy
And I look so small.

Author's journal 2-9-83

Today, Mary Alice took me to a psychic who suggested that

'for the next few years, your life will be like receiving numerous pieces of a jigsaw puzzle in the mail. Some of them won't fit together at all. You will have to trust that they are all part of the same puzzle and they will fit after a while.'

More about radical trust?

Mary Alice later commented wisely, 'Radical trust is a decision.'

Yuk.

Journal excerpt
Minneapolis, MN October 10, 1982

....

Resistance as a Compost Heap
(or fertiliser that used to be garbage.)

> The Discount Hierarchy, developed by Jacqui Schiff, identifies four levels of resistance which need to be explored and overcome before any problem can be effectively addressed.[14] By recognising energy trapped as resistance we can transform it into the energy of action and solution. This model has been used over many years as a Protective Behaviours training exercise, and in recent years has become known as 'The Compost Heap Model'.
>
> When we start trying to solve problems without considering existing resistance, the resistance often goes underground and sabotages our best efforts. We then risk having the buried resistance block our efforts to have effective programs and action from taking root, like a hard clay soil hidden beneath the surface. These

---

[14] The levels are **EXISTENCE**, which denies that there is a problem; **SIGNIFICANCE**, which denies the importance or relevance of the problem; **SOLVABILITY**, which denies that anything can be done about the problem; **SELF**, which denies personal responsibility or ability to do anything about the problem.

four resistance levels form a hierarchy so that previous levels of resistance must be discarded before moving onward. Hence the analogy of the Compost Heap. As the garbage of a previous resistance level is moved through and turned into the soil of our work and understanding, it becomes the enriching fertiliser which supports further growth.

Three years ago, our not very supportive Director, in a meeting of School Support Staff, at which I was present, described the Protective Behaviours Program as a 'personality-dependent curriculum' identifying it as an example of less important priorities for school social workers and psychologists. Now the Madison Metropolitan School District is being sued for $600,000 essentially, in the opinion of the lawyers, for failing to provide Protective Behaviours strategies to school children and staff.[15] The Persistence Expectation seems to relate directly to this situation. The children who reported apparently stopped telling when they felt they were believed, rather than persisting until enough happened so that they felt safe. If nothing else, this suit will bring into dialogue children's reporting of their fears and experiences and the importance of taking these reports seriously.

Journal excerpt
November 24, 1983

Anatomy of a Decision - Journal Extracts March 1984 to June 1984

Go for it! ... We did! Protective Behaviours, Inc. is now official. It will take a while longer to get a tax exempt status, but it is only a matter of time - and paper work. Much paper work. Starting a new organization is very papered! Thank goodness for Glenn who is busily writing the by-laws and other procedures we need to be official. I will be Director, Michael, Glenn and Dick Dickman will be board of directors, Mary Alice and Donna will be advisors but declining Board Membership because of distance. So we have a pro-feminist but all male board - interesting that it worked out that way in this budding feminist organization!?

---

[15] The suit was being brought by the family of Paula McCormick, an eleven year old girl who was kidnapped, raped and murdered by a neighbour in April 1983. Although Protective Beheviours was being piloted in a number of Madison schools in 1983, and the then superintendent had made several public statements claiming the program as a district program, it was still essentially up to the initiative of individual school social workers as to whether the PB Program was offered. Lack of organisational support had hindered the implementation of the program on a larger scale. At the time, I was a school-based social worker and did not have any district-wide responsibilities as part of my official job description. The Paula McCormick tragedy was the impetus for Madison school implementing a variant of Protective Behaviours in the fall of 1983. This is a classic example of 'crisis-as-eye-opener' at the significance and solvability levels of the Compost Pile method of dealing with resistance. Isn't it frustrating that we so often have to wait until there is a crisis to get the level of awareness and access to resources that allows effective action?

... It has been an eventful week. Last Sunday night after the long plerk[16] session with the Creative Actions bunch - Michael, Glenn, Mary Alice and Donna - we made a firm decision to incorporate Protective Behaviours as a non-profit organization and to reduce my time in the schools still further. (Last year I cut back to half time.) Then, only two days later, on Tuesday morning, Fran Nelson from Parental Stress called asking if PB was a non-profit and if so would I be interested in joining a coalition developing a grant proposal to the United Way! Glenn had just made out the non-profit organizational papers the day before and was filing them that very morning! So I said yes, rather breathlessly. There are four other agencies considering a large-visioned prevention effort and our first meeting will be Friday. They are talking about $200,000 over two years of which at least $30,000 would come to Protective Behaviours Inc. the first year. What a surprise, a wonderful surprise. When I told Glenn his comment was -

> 'Of course! That's just the beginning. We've now made room for support to come to us.'

I trust he's right. Radical trust is a decision, hmmm?

March 14, 1984

Today I had a conversation with 'Old Peg' my inner elder. I've been reading Virginia Woolf's A Writer's Diary, in which she comments that she writes her journal in the context of imagining an older self, 'Old V.' who will be reading the writing of her younger self at a later date. So, I thought I would try it.

What a surprise! I pictured the most positive scenario I could imagine - Old Peg is sitting up there in the future, looking back over a life well lived, feeling well cared for, looking back with considerable satisfaction. I imagined her sitting in a beautiful outdoor place, a few months before our death. I asked her what she thought about all this - should I take a full time leave, go all out for Protective Behaviours, Inc. or was it too risky? After all, I figured, it's the security of her future, too, that I'm risking.

Well, she doesn't have any doubts about what I should do!

> 'Go for it - *QUIT* your job,' she told me without hesitation. 'Now, looking back, what I need is interesting memories - not regrets. So what if it doesn't work out? What would be hard for me, up here in the future, would be wondering what would have happened if you _hadn't_ gone for it. Or worse yet, that you didn't and someone else had!'

---

[16] Plerk is a favourite PB term for work that is combined with play, so that much is achieved with the maximum of enjoyment.

'But ... but ...,' I interjected, 'What about retirement monies, and medical insurance, and ...'

'Never mind about that - my needs now are not many. I have all I need. Living your life fully and adventurously is the best gift you can give me. And you've done pretty well so far! Go for this one. Anyhow, if you stay in the schools, you'll have medical insurance to pay for the skin cancer treatments, but if you leave you may just not have cancer - have you considered that?'

Whew - I was certainly surprised - somehow I had bought into the idea that I would get more conservative, less adventurous as I got older. Seems like that's not necessarily so! Old Peg may be a useful guide - I think I'll consult her more often. (An inner elder! who is to me now as I am to my inner child?)

QUIT my job? Whew! That feels scary. But I could take an unpaid year's leave.

April 2, 1984

The Coalition grant is done and turned in. Scuttlebutt has it that it is being well received. It should be - some very creative work has gone into it. If we get it, it would pay my salary for a full year, maybe two, and probably provide basic operating expenses for a Protective Behaviours office. We'll be notified of the decision by July 15. That's the exact same date that I'll have to let the schools know if I'm taking a year's leave of absence without pay. So it's all working out.

May 10, 1984

School is out! Summer's here. I'm happy as usual about the free time looming ahead - one of the perks of working in the schools - summers off. Yet I feel like my life is on hold until July 15 when the decision about the grant proposal will be made - and the latest that I can let the schools know if I'm going to do that instead next year. It is hard to be in the present when I don't know what I'll be doing next year - and don't have any control over what the United Way decides ...

June 8, 1984

It's not working - I've been obsessing about the decision whether or not I'll be taking a leave next year, and feeling powerless. I do want to see if I can make a living doing just Protective Behaviours, instead of just fitting it into my spare time. I want it to be prime time, and am close to deciding it is time to step off the cliff. Even if the United Way Grant doesn't come through, I'm pretty sure I want to do this. My inner elder, Old Peg, is cheering me on - no resistance from her - quite the opposite!

June 14, 1984

Enough already! Time to risk and adventure! So today I went down to the school administration building and told them I had decided to take a leave next year. As I was leaving the building, fait accompli, past the point of no return (well, not for a year anyway,) I felt terrific! I had, and still have, a distinct physical sensation of steel bands coming off my head, and my thoughts ranging more widely. In fact, some of the ideas which I have been used to having contained, went careening off practically across the horizon. For instance, I could go away to a warmer place for a month or more next winter - I don't have to stay in the Wisconsin winter. For a month or more?!

(undated in June 1984)

Daughters

Approaching cronehood in May - my 56th birthday - and apparently now post-menarche. No periods for a long time ... 8 months ... 10 months. I am aware of new directions, options eliminated as new paths open.

I will never have a birth daughter in this life. There is deep sadness in that for me. As a youngest daughter, of a youngest daughter, of a youngest daughter, of a youngest daughter, I feel an ending of a cycle. (Moving just a bit sideways the cycle continues through my sister's children - my niece Margaret, my sister's youngest daughter, and Meg, my other niece Tora's youngest daughter - me to niece to grandniece, all Margarets.) Oh yes, I can Polly Anna it out with ideas of daughters of my children ... but grandmother is not an imminent role, nor may it loom large in my later life.

The turning to the work in the fullest sense of the vision is a way (a crone's way?) of cutting some threads, and enlarging the cycle ... Protective Behaviours speaks so directly to the little sisters, the youngest daughters, the big sisters, adult women in the roles of mother, aunt, grandmothers or un-childed but birthing the world in other ways.

Protective Behaviours is my daughter (in much the same way my mother's unwritten books were her children that she sometimes worried about losing in her last days - until she symbolically gave them to me). A daughter of my own, who will care for me as I age ... a tigery, compassionate, feminist daughter. What a nourishing idea!

Journal excerpt
March 24,1984

More on daughters. When my father died ten years ago, I felt a great increase in my ability to self-nurture ... awareness of being my own daughter. I have also experienced some of that following my mother's death last year, but not so strongly - perhaps because of the 'birth' of the Protective Behaviours vision?

Journal excerpt
March 26,1984

Youngest Daughter

I am the youngest daughter
Of a youngest daughter, Florence
Of a youngest daughter, Ruthette
Of a youngest daughter, Catherine.

Catherine Flandreau was her name.
I never knew her,
But I am her name.
Through me this youngest daughter spiral
Cycles, sweeps and widens.

For I, a crone now, fifty-six
Have no daughter in this lifetime,
No youngest daughter
Of this flesh,
To spiral strongly on.

So, instead, I choose
All children as daughters,
Including the inner girlsprites
Within us each.

And so also choose myself
The small girl child within
As daughter and companion.

My pledge to you girlspirits
Alive now, past and yet to be
To us all, myself included is

To protect and celebrate
Trust and cherish
Revelling in our adventuring.

Each of us a youngest daughter
Cherishing our inner selves
As youngest daughters,
Of youngest daughters
Of youngest daughters
Treasured.

Through us this daughter spiral
Cycles, sweeps and widens
        An evolving, twirling
        Un ending legacy.

CHAPTER 8

AUSTRALIA CALLING - AND THEN WHAT?

I was sitting on the pier, enjoying a break in the warm September afternoon, wondering whether this Protective Behaviours venture was going to work, when Glenn called out of the window that someone in Australia wanted to talk with me. I rushed up the three flights of stairs, breathlessly called the international operator, and a few minutes, and many miles later, I was talking to Vicki Brown, then Police Sergeant in Melbourne Australia. During this phone call I learned that our Protective Behaviours Process had been selected for piloting after a world search of more than a hundred and twenty child safety programs by the Melbourne Crime Prevention Education Consultancy Group, (CPECG). And I didn't even know that a copy of our materials had gone to Australia. The Australian adventure had begun. And what an extraordinary adventure it was to be!

The Australian adventure deserves a whole book of its own, and I am still too close to it to summarize it well. After that initial phone call, one thing led to another, and in April 1985, I travelled to Australia, sponsored by the CPECG, to conduct training sessions in Melbourne, Adelaide and Sydney - about five hundred people in half a dozen sessions. During that short time, I met many people who became friends, colleagues and PB advocates. Talking with people eager to hear about our developments and experience with Protective Behaviours, and who thought, most of them, that it was the best of programs in the world, was gratifying to say the least. Coming after the resistance I had encountered in implementation at home, it was like expecting a mickey mouse watch for my birthday and instead getting all of Disneyland! Only a year or so earlier I had thought that I would go on being a school social worker for five or ten more years and then slip quietly into retirement. Little did I know that the world had such wonderful plans in store for me.

I learned such a lot on the first trip to Australia, and it was a strong impetus to internalize the program still more deeply personally. What a fertile context to further develop the Protective Behaviours Process in joint problem-solving with Australians. An international network. I wrote the following in my journal of the on the trip home after that first training trip.

....

I'm writing this on the plane returning to the US from Melbourne, at the end of my first Protective Behaviours trip, just having been seen off by Vicki and Pam. Much as I am now eager to be home again, leaving Australia is hard ... I have had much plerk and learning here. And connections with remarkable people - Vicki, for one of many ... So the first Australian adventure is beginning to go into the past. Did it really happen or is it all a dream? When I get home, how will I know? Yet I know that looking at a world map will never be the same for me. I'm remembering the world maps I saw in the tourist shops with Australia at the top of the map - 'Australia: No Longer Down Under'. The three specific sites of my visits glow warmly in my remembering now - Melbourne, Adelaide, Sydney.

... I have felt and heard the eloquence that grows out of the process grow in me, and hear that eloquence, excitement and enthusiasm coming back at me - not only from those at home, Michael, Glenn, Michal, Lorraine, but from Australians now - dozens, hundreds. And people with in-depth grasp of the process on a personal level using it as well to confront resistance continually, effectively. Such clarification of our work. I feel my own clarity increasing.

I'm feeling very satisfied, yet also sad, suspended and very tired.

Journal excerpt
May 11, 1985

May 15, 1985, my fifty seventh birthday. Just back from my first trip to Australia ... readjustment, imbalance. The wider vision persists, and I am impatient with those who don't share it ... they've never shared it. Just now my commitment to Protective Behaviours International is great and recently fertilized, and the discrepancy here is particularly noticeable. And frightening, to be honest. It is lonely when I let myself realize how few people can know what this means to me. I know how powerful this program can be ... and is already to some extent. But it is not happening here ... here is where I want it to happen more. And today I learned that only half of the Madison Schools have continued to implement even the watered down version of Protective Behaviours. I feel weird and crazy. Sometimes I see the way clearly and confidently, and sometimes I feel inept and confused and angry. Digging in the garden helps. This may be the year of the garden, by necessity, as I need to garden for sanity!

Tonight Glenn cooked a magnificent birthday dinner - apricot-apple glazed chicken, asparagus with some exotic sauce, herbed rice, and to top it off, cake with strawberries, chocolate mousse icing and whipped cream. Surrounded by my friends, flowers and presents, I collapsed gratefully into the celebratory intimacy. This too is real, not just the discouragement I'm feeling so strongly right now. <u>This</u> is the real world. Not a bad life! Underlying it all is the deep satisfaction of being able to do my work. Right livelihood, as the yogis would put it. Not many people get to do the thing they think is the most important thing they know how to do, and have it be their central life work. I'm very grateful that I get to do this.

Journal excerpt

Sitting on the pier this afternoon, taking a break, I suddenly felt homesick for Australia. <u>Homesick</u> for Australia, what a strange mix up of feelings. Australia is certainly a home for Protective Behaviours, a more spacious, gracious and welcoming home than we've been able to build as yet here. It's tempting to idealize, especially as the difficulties are more apparent to me here at home. Deep feelings of scare right now regarding the reduced funding from United Way, our major funder last year. It will be only $10,000 rather than the $20,000 we'd requested. How dare they? Don't they know that some people think this is the best program in the world? Apparently not.

I'm frightened, too, about the lawsuit that Paula McCormick's family is bringing against Madison School District. (I'm eating my fried rice very fast as I write this.) The McCormick's attorney, Bob McCormick seems to feel that establishing me as an expert and fact witness will cause the School District to settle out of court. I had not realized that he considered my involvement that crucial, but he does seem to think so, and is putting in considerable time coaching me on courtroom skills. The fact remains that I am willing to testify, and this may be burning bridges.

> Journal excerpt
> undated July? August? 1985

I awoke this morning anxious, and spent ten minutes figuring out how to pay bills I've already paid! This suddenly seemed a familiar feeling, but I had never recognized it so blatantly before. Financial harassment. If someone else asked payment for bills already paid I would be annoyed and expect an apology for financial harassment. Yet that is what I am doing to myself! I became startled and annoyed ... and somewhat distrustful of my own perceptions. (This may be a good feeling to remember and recognize - feelings of distrust and uncertainty as a reaction to internal harassment?) I recalled several similar early mornings when I had 'forgotten' about loans due me ... or other income pending.

Now engrossed in this analysis, I have burned the toast!

> Journal excerpt
> February 2, 1985

Today in the mail there was a large brown envelope with a return address simply, 'The White House'. In it was an official-looking certificate, signed by the President of the United States, commending Peg Flandreau West (me!) for ' ... outstanding contributions to the safety of America's children.' Enclosed also was a signed letter from President Reagan with more of the same, and thanking me on behalf of America's children.

And what a welter of feelings have been running through me since I opened the envelope this morning. I'm appalled. Yes, glad for the recognition, yet angry and sad, too. I feel like crying. In frustration? And no doubt the newspapers will call, and what will I say? What needs to be said is that I am being commended for a program that may be withering away from lack of support. This is the kind of program that the Reagan policies and economics have been undercutting. Reagan has done more than any president in my memory to lessen the safety not only of children, but of all of us. He's carefully not made the connections between child abuse, woman abuse and the militarization of this country and the increasing deficit that will result in even more pull backs on human services. This certificate seems such an empty gesture. Maybe I could respond by saying that I shook the envelope but the $100,000 cheque did not fall out. Had they neglected to enclose it?

I'm also horrified. I don't see this as an honour - it seems like an attempt to lull us into complacency, yet my honest reaction seems churlish. I feel like I want to wash my hands.

It's a very large certificate - and my office walls are so small, and so is our budget and bank account.

Duane just stopped by and commented - 'If Reagan had any idea what you are doing, Peg, he never would have sent you a certificate commending you!'

I could hang it upside down as a signal of distress!

I'm a little startled at how appalled and angry I feel.

Journal excerpt
September 14, 1987

Today is Mother's birthday - she would have been 98. I sent spring flowers to Bette - 'Happy Mother's Birthday! If it weren't for this day we wouldn't have been sisters. I'm certainly glad I didn't miss <u>that</u>!

This has been a long difficult week of discouragement, cancelled trainings and financial worries. Then this morning - an additional bummer. Skin cancer check-up confirmed three more suspicious lesions on my face that need surgery. Considerable pressure to have them done today, but I decided to wait until after the Two Day Intensive Training on April 4th and 5th so as to have some free non-public time for the three weeks of bandages and healing. Now I realize there are several workshops in April also. Perhaps best I have the lesions taken care of sooner? Yuk! What is the meaning of all this? More practice in maintaining equilibrium in the midst of difficulties? Need for less dependence on physical appearances ... physical reality? Need for less emphasis on being in the public eye ... or making more connections between this violation of bodily well-being and other victimization? More learning about what to do about anger when there is no one to be specifically angry at? Certainly application to the political context there ... lack of adequate funding for PB, no medical insurance etc. etc. Perhaps when I am eighty it will all become clear. Right now it is not. I don't have time or finances to take three weeks off right now, nor do I want to invest the energy it takes to get through the pain and convalescence.

I again find myself thinking that this would be as good a time as any to have a fatal 'accident'. I wonder what would happen to PBI, to Dave and others, the Rutledge Street house? It's very tempting ... life seems hard and effortful right now. I'm tired. I don't want to gear up for more face pain. I don't want to deal with the financial difficulties any more. I don't like it that there will not be another trip to Australia this year.

But if I left now it would be a mess. I should make a will. (Is this one reason I have been putting that will off ... because I can't leave until I have that in place? Hmmm.) What if this mood of despair doesn't lift?

I do know how to work through this view to the other side, but am stubbornly reluctant to use what I know this morning. 'Do a gratitude litany,' I tell myself impatiently, ... and dig my heels in. NO! I don't want to feel grateful, I want to have a tantrum. I want it *my* way, or I don't want to play anymore. My inner elder smiles quietly.

> 'Lots of luck!' she comments, 'That's not the way it works in this life.'

> 'Oh shut up ... Who asked you?' I counter grumpily.

But it is all beginning to seem a bit ludicrous ... now I'm angry about other options coming into focus! Here I am defensively fighting against being alive. Sometimes I *hate* being resilient and buoyant!

I am further reminded by the oaks outside my window - I'm writing this at the lakeside terrace of the University of Wisconsin Union - of Marge Piercy's poem, *The Doughty Oaks*.[17]

> 'Oaks don't drop their leaves ... leaves hang on withering, tougher than leather ... they give up nothing willingly ... in the spring how stubborn, how cautious, clutching their wallets tight ...'

---

[17] Marge Piercy 'The Doughty Oaks' in *The Moon is Always Female*. Alfred A. Knopf, New York, 1980.

It's March here now and these oaks still have their last year's leaves. Me too, resisting the new growth cycle, challenges. These oak trees, deep rooted, now surrounded by cement circles, stand in silent denial of death, in affirmation of dormancy and holding on to old leaves as part of a natural cycle during times of little nourishment. They seem to be smiling compassionately, patiently inviting me to share their view of the world.

No ... I don't want to! Stamp!! Stamp!!

Journal excerpt
March 4, 1987

Editor's note:

The above extracts from Peg's diary give an indication of some of the challenges which she faced in pursuing her dream and her life's work. It was not all plain sailing by any means. However the discouragement which she felt at times never deterred her from her goal. In a letter she sent to us soon after the Gulf War had begun, Peg wrote,

'I came across a quotation in my readings recently that has stayed with me. I've been feeling considerable discontent and deep discouragement that we have not been able to engage our leaders in willingness to find non-violent solutions, and that our US President and military forces are now engaging in violence again. But the quotation - from Krisnamurti:

> *"As you grow older," (and I would add ... and in troubled times,) "keep your discontent alive with the vitality of joy and affection. Then that flame of discontent will have an extraordinary significance because it will build, create, it will bring new things into being."*

It seems to me that's what we're doing. I am glad we in PB are choosing to acknowledge our discontent with the way things are and are spending our time and energy mainly constructively on those things that make for peace. I am grateful ... for the opportunity to do this work ...'

At that time she was looking forward with great eagerness to her third visit to Australia to participate in the 5th Protective Behaviours National Conference with the theme, Living Without Violence : Let's Talk About It. It was a visit Peg was never to make. However the following extract from her journal, written after her second Australian visit, gives an indication of the warmth and encouragement she felt at that time.

My eyes teared up with happiness as I stood savouring a moment I knew that I would remember all the rest of my life. It is not always that I recognize, at the very happening, a time that will be a memory-source of encouragement and gratitude. This one I recognized easily and it remains always fresh and alive. Especially now as I write, I am aware of pre-tears and a flooding of appreciation and gratitude, a shining feeling-memento of that moment in Adelaide, Australia.

I was in attendance at the second Annual Protective Behaviours <u>National</u> Conference. Just knowing that the first Annual Conference had been held the previous year, with representatives from all the Australian states and territories, had been an incredible excitement for me from a distance. And now, almost unbelievably, I was present, actually there at the second. I was a part of an actual gathering of many people who were working to further my ideas in Australia. It was a sparkling experience - more so than even I had anticipated. I frequently felt unable to contain the excitement I felt, and the affection, appreciation and attention I was being invited to receive.

The Conference had assembled in the large conference room at the Arkaba Hotel in Adelaide. Representatives from <u>all</u> the Australian states and territories were present. Ever since I had arrived, I had been reconnecting with old friends and acquaintances and friends from my first visit three years earlier, and putting faces to correspondents, telephone friends and others. The Conference had been skillfully, meticulously and playfully planned, and I was already having a wonderful time. As I looked around the room, I felt a deep sense of community and the potential of many shared adventures. And then this moment.

Sue Gordon finished her spirited introduction of me by saying that her life had been changed by my ideas and her continuing work with internalizing the Protective Behaviours Process. A lump formed in my throat. I already had considerable respect for Sue's perceptive analysis, and this personal tribute was uniquely meaningful to me. However, she did not stop there - she suggested that there were others who had also had similar experiences with the Protective Behaviours Process. She then invited anyone in the audience who felt their lives had changed as a result of internalizing the Protective Behaviours Process to raise their hands.

To my elation and enchantment, the room became a sea of hands. I saw them then through a film of tears as I stood and heard the applause break out. I stood for a long moment savoring that instant. I knew I would always remember and often revisit it.

For those of you, reading this now, who were in that audience, I thank you again. What an incredible moment for my life's memory to contain! Thank you for giving it to me.

....

CHAPTER 9

SUCCESS STORIES FROM AND ABOUT OTHERS

A Native American woman gathers visible Network support

In one Protective Behaviours Training in a northern Wisconsin community, a majority of the participants were Winnebago Native Americans. At one point in the session, while we were discussing networking and the use of resources, a Native American woman stood up. She spoke of difficulties with equitable law enforcement, and issues of trust. She cited several instances of white police officers either not responding to domestic violence calls, or showing up and over-reacting using verbal abuse and undue force while arresting Native American men. This caused a dilemma for Native American battered women who attempted to obtain police protection from violence. The women themselves were concerned about the racial basis of the abuse the Native American men often received at the hands of the police, and often felt even more vulnerable when the men returned, bruised and humiliated - and even more angry at the woman who had involved the police. Often, the speaker commented, the tribal elders and other members of the tribe felt that such matters should be handled through the Tribal Councils, and frequently were perceived as being prejudiced against the women who attempted to gain white police protection.

While she was talking, several other Native Americans, men as well as women, quietly stood and remained standing. I too, remained standing and quiet, thinking over what she had said. Then, realizing that the five others were still also on their feet, I asked slowly, somewhat puzzled as they did not take a turn to speak,

>'What's happening now?'

>'We're standing with her,' one of the women answered.

The first speaker looked around, and apparently satisfied, sat down. At which point the others sat down also.

Later I wondered, a one-step removed 'what if.' What if we all started doing this. What would our world be like if we did? What if we all, literally, started standing in support when we agree or are interested, sitting only when we disagree or are bored? It could be somewhat disconcerting for speakers to have such immediate and honest feedback, and it might make all speeches, especially political ones, shorter.

....

'Somehow I did persist!'

'Looking back on it now, it doesn't seem like such a big deal, but at the time it was. I'm thirty years old, manic depressive, and sometimes I get crazy. Not just manic acting, but very fast inside, too. Like I can't think straight because my brain speeds up and too much is going on all at once.

At first it feels sort of good - I have lots of energy, I don't need much sleep, and I feel like I can do most things more easily. It's like a natural high. But then it gets to be too much, too fast and if I don't get some help, then it all snowballs and I end up in the hospital. Sometimes I haven't gotten into the hospital until after quite a while of being very crazy on the streets.

I'm very responsible about taking Lithium when I'm not manic - but when I start getting manic, I honestly don't know what I do. Perhaps sometimes I forget to take it, or sometimes I take extra. Time just gets different for me then, and it's hard to keep track of even simple things.

I haven't been able to figure out yet why I break through and get manic sometimes even when I'm taking my meds regularly. And the doctors don't seem to be able to figure it out either.

When I'm manic, I don't think anyone else knows anything, I don't want any advice, and I don't think anyone is trying to help me, even if they are. When I start to get manic it feels so great that I just like to be that way for a while. And like I said, sometimes then I start to feel like other people are just interfering in my life, and I get annoyed even with the people who I usually know have my best interests at heart. It doesn't feel to me like help at that point, it feels bothersome, and I just want them to go away and leave me alone to run my own life. And I tell them that.

I've been dealing with this condition since I was nineteen - I'm thirty now - and I've learned a lot about it myself. I can tell now when I start to go up - there are signs, if I can let myself notice them. It's hard, like I said, because it feels so good to have lots of energy again. But when I start sleeping less, that's an early sign, and so is the feeling that my brain is speeding up. I think that's my Earliest Warning Sign - my brain speeding up. But that's hard to notice sometimes, because at first I just think I'm having an especially good day. And another and another ...

Well, this last time when I started to get manic, I did something different. I hadn't been sleeping, and I was speeding up inside fast. I was getting very short tempered with people around me. And I realized that I needed to get some attention, and I needed it fast. Sirens in my head. Well, I called my Doc for an appointment, and the receptionist said, 'Next week.'

I just hung up, mad, because I needed it sooner than that, and somehow I didn't have the patience right then to explain to her.

Now other times when this has happened, I've just gone off and been mad, let myself feel that no one wants to help me, and then pretty soon I'm thinking no one <u>can</u> help me, and then I get farther into the manic and think I don't <u>need</u> any help.

But this time I didn't do that. Somehow I did persist - and I realized that I didn't have much time. It was an emergency for me. More sirens in my head. I realize now, looking back, that I was already thinking skewed - I never even considered going to my social worker. But never mind that - I did what I needed to do as I saw it then.

So I went to my Dad's office, and he was out just then. He was in town, and that was lucky - because he travels a lot. So, I just paced around in his office, and waited until he came back. I told him I needed to be in the hospital, and he seemed to agree because he made some phone calls and got it arranged for me. I guess it was simple for him - but it didn't seem simple to me at the time, it seemed very hard and complicated. Partly because my brain was going a hundred miles an hour, and I couldn't stay on one thought for more than a short time.
As it turned out, I <u>was</u> right, I did need to be in the hospital - and it took a while to get back in balance again. Looking back, I feel like I made a good decision, to decide that I knew what I needed, instead of waiting until I got so crazy-acting on the streets that the cops would take me in. Now I think I'll probably be able to take care of myself just as well the next time - and maybe sometime there will be a way to cure manic-depression. I sure hope so, and I hope it's soon.'

> Dave R. West
> as told to the author
> June 1988

.....

Carmen refers a friend

Carmen, an eleven year old incest survivor, brought a classmate up to me in the school hallway one day.

> 'Peg knows all about my father,' she said by way of introduction. 'And she helped me and my Mom. You can talk to her about what's happening to you.'

> Incident at Schenk Elementary School
> Madison, Wisconsin (USA)
> February 1980

....

Verbal self empowerment in action

An older woman acquaintance of the author was enjoying a birthday celebration. As the blazing many-candled birthday cake was brought in, a nice-young-man, attempting to compliment the celebrant, commented,

> 'There must be some mistake! You can't be that old. This must be the wrong cake!'

The Birthday Woman, paused for a moment and surveyed the many candles accurately depicting her age as she had requested. Looking up at the would-be well wisher, she replied radiantly,

> 'Please don't deprive me of my age. I have earned it.'

Later she told me this was a comment made by one of Isak Dinasen's characters in a similar situation.[18]

Helen Larrimore's response in a similar situation was 'How dare you?!!'[19]

Gloria Stienam also had a reframing comeback, when a well-wisher gave her the lead line, 'You don't look forty.' Her retort: 'This is what forty looks like!'

....

She hadn't seen him for several years. They had been lovers a few times when she was into the singles scene, before she moved away. Lots had happened in the meanwhile, not the least of which was her considerable gain in self confidence, both personally, and as a competent professional. So it felt very familiar, but almost annoying when he greeted her, obviously on the make, with,

> 'Hi Goodlooking!'

No name, no tentativeness, a rather arrogant assumption that she would still be flattered by his attention. His eyes did a slow lingering, 'admiring' body scan.

She wasn't interested in reclaiming this acquaintance she realized, somewhat surprised, for she had been complimented by his attention three years ago. Now his approach, no different than it always had been, seemed so insinuatingly intimate, so ... so ... sexist. She'd not thought him particularly sexist when she was involved with him, but somehow now she was seeing him differently.

> 'You're looking good June!' he continued. 'Looks like you've lost a few pounds ...' Again the suggestive body scan, lingering. He reached out, inviting a hug.

---

[18] The author has been unable to locate the specific situation in Dinasen's writings. It is however, also quoted and attributed to Dinasen in May Sarton's *Journey of a Solitude*.

[19] Helen Larrimore is a feminist therapist in Chicage Illinois and Spring Green Wisconsin.

> 'Oh! No!' She acted startled, patting her hips, her face. 'Not again! I wonder where I lost those pounds this time? I've got to find them right away! Bye now.'

And she left.

Anon. as told to author
December 1979

....

'White sheep of the family.' Racial harassment interrupted.

Odell Taliaferro, eighty three at the time of this writing, has been an articulate activist for many years. The following happened a number of years ago while he was Chair of the local National Association for the Advancement of Colored People (NAACP). The position he held at the University, supporting the professors in their lectures and demonstrations, had increased both in time and responsibilities over the years. Odell Taliaferro was usually sought out by new faculty members for help and suggestions in designing their lecture demonstrations for the basic science courses.

In the months prior to the following incident, several of the new, younger faculty had advocated for his reclassification as faculty specialist, rather than the lower paid technical classification he held. This advocacy had elicited some opposition from several of the more conservative senior faculty. Although race was never mentioned publicly, he <u>was</u> the only black in the department and some others, non-blacks, in other departments, also without PhDs, had already been reclassified as faculty specialists. Eventually the newer faculty won, he was reclassified as faculty specialist, receiving a substantial well-deserved raise. However several of the older men held some resentment about it.

This came out in subtle ways, and was sometimes insidious. For instance, one of Taliaferro's relatives, with the same surname, had gotten into considerable difficulty with the police. The local paper had carried the story on the front page. The following day, Odell Taliaferro happened to be in a crowded elevator with a couple of the senior faculty men.

> 'Oh! Tally!' one of them commented, in pseudo-friendly tones, 'That relative of yours ... he's in considerable trouble again isn't he? That doesn't do much for your NAACP campaign for first class citizenship for colored people, now does it?'

The elevator arrived at Odell Taliaferro's floor. He turned to face his colleagues as he got off.

> 'Yes, he is in trouble again,' he responded, just as the door was closing,
'He's the white sheep of our family.'

as told to the author
Madison Wisconsin (USA)

' ... Maybe later'

Doris, a small, delicate-looking kindergarten girl, had thick, long hair that came almost to her waist - just the kind of hair you wanted to go over and stroke. One of her classmates, Chris, did that.

> 'Don't do that!' she said, and he started to mimic her.

The teacher walked over and said quietly,

> 'That's right, Doris, you don't have to let anyone touch your hair if you don't want them to.'

Then turning to Chris, she added,

> 'Chris, you need to ask Doris if you want to touch her.'

Chris turned to Doris,

> 'Can I touch your hair? It feels like my cat.'

Doris paused a moment and then responded,

> 'Not right now, maybe later.'

And the two went off to play together.

Incident at Kennedy School
Madison, Wisconsin (USA)
September 1983

....

The night Nicky wouldn't cuddle

Jody, seven years old, had had a long day. It had been mostly a good day, but toward the end things had gotten a bit bumpy. Jody was secretly glad when it was time for bed. She cuddled with her mother Carol for a bit, and then settled down in bed for a drowsy cuddle with her cat, Nicky. But Nicky had other ideas. He clearly didn't feel sleepy or cuddly. So he left, and Jody felt lonely. Tired, sleepy and lonely. She tried cuddling her teddy bear. But he wasn't warm and alive. She tried her pillow, then her doll. They just weren't right. She wanted something warm and alive, and she was too tired to pretend. So she went and found Nicky again, stroked his flame-colored fur lovingly and brought him back to her bed. But no, Nicky still wasn't ready to cuddle in. Jody wanted to be asleep, but she wanted a warm alive cuddle, too.

Finally, very quietly, she got up and went into the living room where Carol was grading exams. Carol looked up surprised. Jody usually fell right to sleep quickly when she went to bed. Jody started to say that she was hungry, but then she just blurted out about needing a warm alive something to cuddle with, and how Nicky wouldn't stay and the other things she'd tried just weren't right. Her mother looked thoughtful.

'Would a Mother do?' she asked.

Relieved, Jody climbed up on the couch where her mother had made room for her.

'Can you come into _my_ bed?' Jody asked.

'No, I have to get these exams done. But if it would help, you can cuddle up and go to sleep here beside me while I work.'

So Jody curled her small body up, warm and contented, and was soon asleep. When she woke up the next morning, she was in her own bed, with Nicky curled asleep beside her.

> as told to author by Carol Ziesemer,
> parent and Social Work Field Instructor
> University of Wisconsin
> Madison, Wisconsin, USA
>
> reviewed and okayed by Jody Ziesemer
> who reminded author that Nicky is a 'he'.

Exceptions to the rules, being allowed special treats - these are the moments we may remember with pleasure from our own childhoods. Yet sometimes as parents we hesitate to act on our own best knowledge.

In this situation, Carol didn't immediately assume that this would be the beginning of a dreaded 'Bedtime Problem'. She noticed Jody had made several attempts to solve the problem herself, so she offered an option that might fit both their immediate needs, holding to the reasonable boundary of continuing her work when Jody suggested another option. Jody got the body comfort she knew she wanted, and Carol got to combine mothering and profession to the enhancement of both.

....

Hot chocolate and books - a police officer nourishes her Kidself

Terry was a police officer, a job that she liked pretty well. She lived by herself and usually liked that too, but lately she'd been feeling depressed and bored. Boring, too. Low energy, lots of procrastination. The small child within her seemed to be huddled up in a dark corner.

Passing the public library on her way home from work one afternoon, she suddenly had an idea.

'Why not?' she thought, and a few moments later was talking to the Children's Librarian.

'What books would you recommend for a little girl who doesn't feel special?'

'How old is she?' asked the Librarian thoughtfully, 'And does she have any special reasons for feeling that way?'

'She's about seven,' Terry answered from deep inside herself, 'And, well, she's lonely, she doesn't have a best friend right now, and she feels nobody pays much attention to her. And she's sort of bored.'

It was all true, too, Terry realized. All except being seven. But sometimes she felt that young, like now.

'Sounds like you know her pretty well. She's fortunate to have a friend like you. I do have several books that she might like. Is she a good reader?'

'Oh yes! But I could also read them to her. She'd like that, too.'

Fifteen minutes later, Terry was on her way, a pile of seven books tucked under her arm.

Popcorn and a peanut butter and jelly sandwich for supper, were followed by a long bath in candle light with so many bubbles they spilled over onto the floor. Then she fixed herself a cup of hot chocolate and carried the pile of books to her bedroom. Curled up cozily in bed, she slowly, and with much expression, read the books aloud to herself. As she read, she was aware of her own kidself contentedly snuggling, savoring the hot chocolate and glowing in the closeness of the story time.

      told to author at Michigan (USA) Womens Music Festival 1986

....

Noon hour is story hour - Kidselves welcome

Massive, grey, square, left-brain and very grown-up looking, the Wisconsin State Office Building sits stolidly marking the southwest boundary of the official state buildings. It is in like company. The other boundary markers are the Post Office, the Courthouse, several banks, and the gold-domed Capitol Building itself.

We all know buildings like this one. Inside, beyond the impressive first floor foyer, brass-fronted elevators and wide marble corridors there is an over-crowded maze, with temporary space dividers delineating the hierarchy of civil service status. Those few people who are high enough on the organizational chart rate offices with windows and doors. Inches are hotly negotiated for in reorganization times, and allotted space shrinks down through shared offices, to partitioned areas with brow-high partitions which tallish people can look over and anyone can hear through, and large unprotected areas with workers pooled in entirely visible and interruptible space.

Many of us have worked in buildings like this. Yet we all know that even in the middle of this unlikely environment, incidents of creativity surface.

A creative, playful persistent woman, only too experienced in establishment environments, attended one of our Protective Behaviours Empowerment Trainings. She began adding our ideas to her own considerable survival knowledge.

> 'I was particularly interested in the Inner Child ideas,' she wrote later. 'And I was beginning to feel overwhelmed by my job. So I decided to bring some of those ideas into my work place to see if my Inner Child could be more comfortable there too. I started bringing in flowers, then some pictures, and made personal phone calls during breaks. They all helped ... some ...'
> 'Then one day talking, one of my co-workers and I had another idea. We decided to bring in some of our favorite children's books and read them to each other over lunch. It started with just the two of us, and now each week there are sometimes fifteen people who bring their lunches and stories to read.'

Such Kidself play *is* contagious. It doesn't take a lot of time, can be done at work, and is some of the best burn-out prevention we know.

....

'But didn't you know I was home?'

I was looking out my living room window watching Kate, my seven year old daughter, swinging by her two hands from a tree branch in the front yard. A twelve year old neighbour, a new boy in the neighbourhood, rode up. Jumping off his bike, he ran up to Kate swinging in the air, grabbed her shorts, and pulled them off her dangling legs.

I was about to storm out the front door and accost him, when I noticed that Kate had dropped from the tree, madder than mad, and without even stopping to put her shorts back on, was standing staunchly in her underwear, telling him off in no uncertain terms.

Because it was a hot day with all the windows open, I could hear her singing part of the song they use with the Protective Behaviours Program at her school, 'My body's nobody's body but mine ... I run my body, you run yours.'[20] As she sang she used the gestures taught with the song, and did it have an effect!

The older boy, surprised, cringed away, got back on his bike and rode quickly off

---

[20] *My Body* by Stuart Alsop

without a backward look. Kate stood, hands on hips, until he was out of sight, and then, almost as an afterthought, picked up her shorts and put them back on.

Then she stood thoughtful for a moment, and looked down at her outspread fingers.

> 'Oh good!' I thought, 'She's remembering her Network, and now she's going to come and tell me.'

Kate looked at her hand for a moment longer, and then ran, not indoors to me, but next door to the neighbour's house!

Startled, I wondered why she hadn't felt she could come and tell me. I fixed myself a cup of very strong tea, and sat down to deal with those ever present doubts mothers are prone to.

> 'Didn't I let her know clearly enough that nothing was too awful to tell me ... hadn't I let her know that something like that was not her fault ...?'

I was still buzzing around inside my head a while later when Kate came in. She was humming to herself, and started to get a drink in the kitchen.

Not able to restrain myself, I brought it up myself.

> 'I noticed what happened with that new boy, Kate. That was a terrible thing for him to do and I thought you handled it very well.'

> 'Thanks. He's a pest,' she responded, and settled down with her new library book, drink in hand.

> 'And I noticed you looked down at your hand. I was wondering if you were remembering your Network then?'

> 'Yep.' She settled into her book.

> 'And, Kate,' I persisted, 'then I saw you run next door. Didn't you know I was home? You could have come and told me.'

Kate looked up surprised, and slightly impatient.

> 'Of course Mum. I knew I could tell you. But at school they told us to check out our Network people. So that's what I did.'

> 'Oh ...' I said weakly, my recent doubts about being a good parent looking foolish even to me.

> 'And Gloria's Mum thought it was awful too. She said I must have told him strongly or he wouldn't have ridden away so quickly. OK?'

That last 'OK' also meant 'Can I read in peace now please?' So I turned away, relieved and not a little chagrined about my own self-hassling. She didn't have to check me out, she knew I'd support her. I also felt a sudden appreciation of the Network idea myself, and decided to let you know about this.

> Barbara Pamphilon, Lecturer in Health Education
> and Kate Pamphilon, PB Practitioner

....

'It would have made such a difference.'

As a partial barter with a doctor friend, I had earlier provided several copies of Safe, Adventurous and Loving,[21] the new Protective Behaviours pamphlet for parents, to the receptionist for the waiting room. As I was leaving after my appointment, she stopped me.

> 'You know ...' she said, holding up the booklet, 'I read the themes on the first page, just the first page, and I felt like crying. This booklet would have made such a difference to me when I was little. Just having someone say that.'

I nodded. She continued,

> 'And I was a reader. If I had seen that lying around, I would have read it. I always like to read things about kids that were meant for grownups.'

> 'Yeah, me too,' I grinned.

> 'Do you think I could have one to have at home, to leave lying around ... just in case? And maybe one to leave in the women's room here at work, too?'

> 'Of course. I handed her the two more I had with me. 'Let me know when you need some more.'

> 'Well,' she said hesitantly, 'I made this list after I read it ... could I have ten?'

> Madison, Wisconsin 1984

....

---

[21] Peg Flandreau West, Safe Adventurous and Loving. Latest edition published by Essence Publications, Adelaide, 1989.

Geelong children carry on creatively

Carol Randall, an educator in Geelong, Australia sent me the following incidents:

Whilst on holidays in a camping area, two girls from my grade were confronted with the problem of an 'undesirable character' in the toilets. These girls had their PB Books with them and within the day had inserviced some twelve children from the campsite, ages ranging from four to sixteen, on the strategies of Protective Behaviours and the group had devised their own network of parents and campers and a set of strategies, including surveillance.

One child (Year 5) informed me that her cousin in a city some seventy kilometres away had told her about a problem which the cousin had regarding abuse. The girl from my room was able to take her Protective Behaviours book[22] to her cousin - inserviced her on PB and the cousin was able to find help and the problem was solved.

Another boy (ten) was having a few problems (minor) at home so decided to run away for a while. He coaxed two other friends to go with him. Hence after school one day they ran off. They were found five hours later by the police. On questioning the next day, I asked why hadn't they used PB. (I was convinced that I had not taught the message correctly!) The reply was

> 'But we took our PB books. We felt safe with them, and knew we could work out any problems we were confronted with.'

They had taken a bag of apples, a blanket ... and their PB books!

A girl (nine):

> 'Mrs. Randall! I have a problem, and I have run out of fingers!'[23]

A brainstorming activity by the other students soon revealed that she also had another hand and two feet! A good lesson for The Persistence Expectation.

....

---

[22] Carol Randall notes, 'The children were provided with a special book in which all discussion summaries, network reviews and theme statements, as well as their own worksheets, group brainstorms and individually chosen networks, were kept as a permanent record.'

[23] In this class the teacher suggested that the children's networks could be depicted as a hand with the four fingers representing the four individually chosen adults.

'That just doesn't feel like loving to us.' Children handle a touching situation by themselves.

My stepdaugher came up to me last month and told me she got an Early Warning Sign whenever she was around her grandfather, her mother's father. She said that sometimes he hugged her too long, and kissed her sloppily. I was mad, and was ready to go and tell him off in no uncertain terms. But our daughter said that at school she'd learned that sometimes you could just tell someone to stop, and she wanted to try that. I reluctantly agreed, still steaming, with her agreeing that if that didn't work she'd let me know.

The very next weekend, we were at a family gathering at Grandpa's, and our daughter and two of her young cousins were there. I was watching closely, you can imagine. Grandpa came over to the three of them and started to hug one.

'Wait a minute Grandpa,' she said. 'We don't like those hard hugs.'

'And we don't like the sloppy kisses, either!' chimed in the second cousin.

Then our daughter added,

'That just doesn't feel like loving to us, Grandpa.'

Grandpa looked thoughtful and a little embarrassed, as the three girls came running over to us.

'There! We told him,' our daughter whispered to me.

A month later when I asked her, she said that he now hugs them 'sideways and carefully' and the sloppy kisses have stopped.

told to author PTA Meeting, Kennedy School
Madison, Wisconsin USA 1982

This is an example of the 'safety-in-numbers' networking that children are experts at.

It is also a clear example of using the Protective Behaviours ideas in the context of power imbalance. All of these girls were young - seven or younger. The Protective Interrupting occurred within a situation of shared support, with a caring adult watching protectively from the sidelines, and the intervention was direct, descriptive and loving. Here the girls honoured and trusted their own perceptions and handled a situation which felt to them to be abusive. Their perceptions were taken seriously by the stepfather, and by the grandfather.

Also, nobody determined whether Grandpa was doing it 'on purpose', or called him a dirty old man. It is possible that he was a lonely, touch-deprived elder, as many of our elders are, or it is also possible that he was continuing a pattern of abusive behaviour. We don't know from this incident. And it doesn't matter. What we do know is that the girls, with support from a caring adult, got the situation stopped - and they didn't have to demolish the relationship with their Grandpa.

Note that the supportive adult did not just agree to let them handle the situation, and then consider it finished. He asked his daughter to give him feedback, and he initiated a check in later on to be sure that things had indeed changed.

As caring adults, effective, empowerment-inviting support can often be as simple as supporting another's perception of their Early Warning Signs, supporting their ideas for action, and checking back regarding the results. Note that this is very different from expecting potential victims to be responsible for stopping their own victimization - and blaming them when they don't.

....

'He drives real reckless.' Problem solving by a ten year old.

John noticed me carrying a pile of books and papers into school one morning and offered to help.

'I had an Early Warning Sign last weekend,' he confided quietly.

'Yes?' I encouraged.

'Well, I was feeling unsafe, and I used my Network,' he continued. Like many third graders, he liked to be precise with words.

'Good for you,' I responded, 'How'd you do that?'

'I was at a big family party at my uncle's house, and my dad had been drinking so much that I didn't want to go home in the car with him. He drives real reckless when he's like that. So I got someone else to drive me home.'

'Good thinking!' I put my arm around him. 'Exactly what did you do?'

'Well, I asked one of my uncles first, but he said he thought it would be better not to make a fuss about it, and he didn't think my dad was _that_ drunk.'

'But _you_ did?'

'Yeah,' John said ruefully. 'I did. I know. So I told my aunt that I was scared to drive with him, and could she just give me a lift - and not make a big deal of it with my father. So she did. I was kind of afraid he might be mad when he got home, and so was she.'

'Was he?'

'Well, I went right to my room and quick got ready for bed like my aunt suggested. When mom came in to say goodnight, I pretended I was almost asleep, so she told my dad I was asleep. Later I heard them fighting again.'

'But you had kept yourself safe John. You took good care of yourself I think.'

John put his arm load of books on my desk and stood thoughtfully, straightening them.

'I wish he'd stop drinking so much, and they wouldn't fight.'

'Yes, me too. I know that's terribly hard for you. And maybe there isn't a lot you can do about them.'
'Mom doesn't like it either.'

'I bet not. Do you think any of them might be willing to talk to you and me together?'

'I dunno,' he sighed. 'I could ask my mom.'

'You could say I suggested it, if you think that would help. We could talk to your mom about <u>her</u> right to feel safe all the time, too.'

'She feels scared when he drives like that.'

'I'm sure she does. I would. And you do.'

'Maybe I will ask her. Gotta go now, or I'll be late.'

'If you want to talk some more, come on back. Tell your teacher I said it was OK. I'll be here all morning.'

'I think I'm OK now. Thanks.'

'I'm glad you told me John. That was skillful taking care of yourself. Seems to me you've learned things that some grown-ups don't know yet.'

'I sure wish they'd learn too. See ya.'

> Incident at Schenk Elementary School
> Madison, Wisconsin USA
> November 1981

....

'I'm gonna go to Gramma's.' Four year old Mona makes a plan.

In a small midwestern town in the United States, Helen I. had been teaching the PBI Process to the children in the day care center where she worked as a teacher. She was particularly concerned about one four-year old girl, Mona, who was in a family where her father drank excessively, and there were violent fights. Mona's

75

mother had more than once been hurt to the extent of needing medical treatment. Mona had talked with some of the day care staff about being scared. Staff attempts to connect Mona's mother with resources had been unsuccessful.

Because of this and other situations, the staff had persistently brainstormed with all the children about how they could keep from getting caught in the middle when grown-ups were fighting, and how they could keep themselves safe if there was a fight.

One morning Mona came in and confided to Helen T.,

> 'There's gonna be a bad fight soon. Prob'ly t'night.'

> 'That's terrible, Mona.'

Mona seemed thoughtful and somewhat sad, then looked up at her trusted teacher and continued,

> 'Yep. But, you know, that's _their_ problem.'

Helen nodded and continued to listen.

> 'And,' Mona continued firmly, 'I'm gonna go to my Gramma's tonight. Will you help me get the number right?'

Helen did, and Mona did, and Gramma said 'Yes.'

Related to author March 1985
near Keshena, Wisconsin USA

Mona was only 4 years old at the time of the above incident. And yes, it _is_ sad and unfair that a youngster has to face this situation - a complex, dangerous situation no child should have to deal with. And Mona's temporary solution was just that - temporary. It is frustrating and saddening for the adults like Helen T. whose best efforts in intervention with Mona's mother were unsuccessful.

Many of us are now working for changes so that the Mona's of the world don't have to face what this small Mona did. However, in the meantime, children like Mona are presently living lives in the midst of violence. Implementing the PBI Process is one important way to work against violence of all sorts.

This incident illustrates that even very young children can sometimes act in empowered ways to obtain respite and emotional support and to increase the visibility of their situations. Note that this perceptive teacher did not try to talk Mona out of her perceptions. She believed her and supported her in doing what she, Mona, wanted to do. Sometimes that's all we can do in the present moment. Having supportive honest Network people who believe you can make a difficult time seem easier - especially when the abusive situation remains unchanged despite our best efforts.

Quick Network Review because I'm in a hurry.

Cathy, a fifth grader, came up to me in the school hallway just as I was leaving, already almost late for a court hearing.

> 'Can I talk to you? It's about not feeling safe.'
> 'Cathy,' I said slowly, taking a deep breath, 'I just can't talk to you now, but it is very important that you feel safe. You almost didn't catch me. Let's pretend you missed me. What would you have done then?'

She paused.

> 'Talk to someone else then, I guess. One of my Network people.'

> 'So who else could that be?' I persisted.

She thought for a moment,

> 'Maybe my Mom, or the Nurse.'

> 'Your Mom or the Nurse. Good thinking. Another?'

> 'Mrs Soucup, our room mother. She listens to kids.'

> 'Does she? Thanks for telling me. I like to know who safe Network people are. Promise me that you'll talk to one of those people today? Or even all three if you have to? Do you need phone numbers?'

> 'Oh! And Nancy Osborne, in the office. She's one of my Network people too. I could talk to her. And I could get Mrs Soucup's number from Nancy. I did that once before.

> 'Good Cathy. Now you have four others just in case. When I come back here tomorrow, let me know what happened, will you?'

> 'I will.'

It took less than two minutes to get Cathy headed toward the help she did, indeed, need, and I was, also responsibly, just on time to the Court Hearing.

....

Valium in the mashed potatoes

A woman with five children went to her doctor with an all too familiar story of violence toward her by her husband in her home. The doctor prescribed valium for her, because in his opinion it was 'her problem'. She took the prescription home, and knowing that it was her husband's problem not hers, fed him valium in his mashed potatoes. This apparently calmed him down somewhat. When the woman and children were finally able to leave, he was left suffering withdrawal from the valium.

Di Margetts
Domestic Violence and Incest Newsletter
May 1987 Carlton, Australia

32,000,000 grocery bags

In early 1985, Michael Biernbaum, Board member of the recently formed Protective Behaviours Inc. was on holiday travelling to San Francisco on a large jet plane. Seated in the center section, five seats wide, he noticed, three seats over, a woman reading Alice Miller's <u>For Your Own Good</u>. Catching her eye, he reached across the two intervening people and handed her some descriptive material about Protective Behaviours.

'I noticed what you're reading, and I think you'll find this of interest.'

She did - and later climbed across the other passengers to talk with him in the aisle. As it turned out she was a director of Public Relations for Safeway Grocery Stores. One thing then led to another. Glenn Halak, then living in San Francisco, did some further negotiating, Michal Osier developed a graphic. In July 1986, 26,000,000 Safeway grocery bags carried a Protective Behaviours message and were distributed in sixteen US states.

Later at a PB Network meeting someone suggested that we hire Michael Biernbaum full time to ride around on airplanes and make contacts. Another noted that Michal Osier's art would be seen by more people in her lifetime, than Rembrandt's was in his!

....

'I went to bed in the bathtub.'

A young child who had been in one of the Protective Behaviours classes recently, came running up to me on the playground.

'You know what?' she started, and continued before I had time to respond except non-verbally, 'Last weekend I had a sitter who tried to help me get undressed when I didn't want him to. Y'know what I did?'

'No, what?'

'Well, I told him three times to stop, I could do it myself - but he didn't. So ... ', she paused dramatically.

'So ... what did you do then?'

'Well, I grabbed my pillow, my blanket and my teddy bear, and I went in the bathroom and locked the door. I went to bed in the bathtub - it was dry and I didn't put any water in it. Then I just ignored him when he tried to get me to come out.'

'And then, when my Mom came home, she asked me why I was sleeping in the bathroom and I told her. She said we'd never have that sitter again. And she's going to call his mother.'

Journal excerpt
April 1979

You're right, it is red!

The three year old girl in the grocery cart behind me in the check out line was stirring up a storm. Her mother was attempting the impossible job of trying to divide her attention between the child in the cart, her slightly older son beside her whining for some candy from the nearby display, and checking to be sure her shopping was complete. As her son reached again for the forbidden candy, she slapped his hand hard. He teared up and retreated into an angry pout. His sister in the cart started to take up his whiny request.

As the mother turned, about to swat the offending child, I caught her eye.

'It's not easy, is it? Gets embarrassing too sometimes!'

She turned to me, startled and somewhat suspicious, then softened.

'Yeah.'

'It's hard work,' I continued. 'I remember some horrendous grocery store scenes when my kids were that age.'

She changed the potential slap into a squeeze.

'Yeah,' she commented, rolling her eyes. 'They're impossible when they're hungry.'

'Go on ahead of me,' I offered as it was my turn, and I pulled my cart aside. 'I've had lunch.'

'Thanks.' The woman smiled fleetingly, and turned to unload her groceries.

'No!' whined the child in the cart.

I turned to her.

'How come you're wearing a green shirt in the grocery store?'

The child looked down at the red shirt she was wearing, and looked back at me with a frown.

'NOT green,' she glared at me.

'Oh, you're right - it's blue. Did your mother say you could wear a blue shirt to the grocery store?'

'NO! Red!'

I pretended to wipe my glasses off and looked more closely.

'Oh! Of course. Now I see. It IS red, you're right. It's my shirt that's green.'

'No!' She stopped glaring and entered the game. 'Yours red!' and she pointed to my blue shirt. 'Your mother not say so!'

'Ah.' I feigned startlement, 'You're right. Red - I can't believe it! I'll change it when I get home. I shouldn't have! Imagine wearing my red shirt right here in the store.'

I fingered my blue shirt.

Their checkout finished, the woman turned to me.

'Thanks.'

Her son standing by her turned to me,

'My shirt is white,' he informed me firmly with a worried look. It was white.

'Yes,' I whispered. 'You're right, it is. And mine is really blue.'

'No!' squealed his sister, 'it's red!'

I grinned at her.

'Bye, red shirt!'

'Bye, blue shirt!' I responded, and she was wheeled off, grinning and waving back at me.

Then when I proffered my ten dollar bill in payment for my groceries, the checkout person said,

'I'm sorry Ma'am. We don't accept blue money here!'

The woman in line behind me chuckled.

'I bet I'm in trouble too. They probably don't take orange money either!'

Willy Street Coop Grocery
Madison (WI) 1983

Offering temporary support as an ad hoc Network person, and spontaneous Protective Interrupting, with a light touch, doesn't always have to take additional time and energy. A fringe benefit is that it often invites out the Kidselves of those around you. Four years later I still get an internal chuckle at that checkout person's comment.

Two young boys teach their mother Protective Behaviours - and she acts

Late in the school year a classroom teacher drew my attention to the fact that two brothers, both in their second year at our school, were often coming to school bruised. Despite the fact that the boys had been taught Protective Behaviours, and both the classroom teacher and I gave them permission and lots of opportunities to disclose, the boys insisted their bruises were accidental. The school year ended without us gaining any more information about their injuries.

I had suspicions that the boys were being abused and resolved to keep a very close eye on them the following year.

However this turned out to be difficult. The boys did not return to our school the next year, and the school records were not transferred, so we had no way of knowing where the boys were.

However, one day I saw the boys' mother at the shopping mall.

> 'Oh!' she said, coming up to me. 'I've been meaning to tell you - you know that de facto of mine? I found out he'd been bashing my boys. I thought something was wrong, but neither of them would say anything to me. So finally I said to them, "You know you told me that teacher at your school says - there's nothing so awful you can't talk with someone about it," - and do ya know they told me about all the times he bashed 'em. And that's why they're not at your school now. I didn't feel safe so I left him, moved, and changed their school so he can't find us.'

Reported by Gwen Gilbert, Educator
Victoria, Australia

....

Rainbows can outlight the movie in my head

Two weeks after we'd done a Protective Behaviours class session on Domestic Violence, 'What if the grown-ups at home were fighting, how could you keep from getting caught in the middle?' - Barb Jung, a skilled, loving and perceptive second grade teacher approached me. She told me that one of her second graders seemed preoccupied. Upon gentle inquiries, the child, Tanya, had expressed worries about her mother's safety.

> 'I told her I thought it would be a good idea if she talked with you,' continued Barb, 'And she remembered you'd said "Nothing is too awful to talk about with someone." So we agreed you might be that someone. She's a bit reluctant, feels disloyal to her Mom, I think, but she said she's willing to talk with you. I know I'd feel better if she did.' (Network support on several levels!)

So Tanya and I had lunch together. She wasn't sure she should be telling anyone, then confided she felt as if she had 'a movie running in my head that I can't turn off.' She kept seeing her Mother's friend bursting noisily in the door, and hurting her mother. Her mother had now told her that she she had broken up with Bill. He had moved out, but that had happened before too, and then they'd made up, he'd come back and hurt her mother again. Her mother said that this time it was different, Bill was going to be gone for good, but how could she be sure?

Tanya and I had lunch again. By this time, Tanya had told her mother that her teacher had noticed how worried she was, that she, Tanya, had talked to me, and wanted her mom to talk to me too. And her mom had agreed. Tanya was an articulate child, with some strong survival skills, and she had a close relationship with her mother.

Tanya made the arrangements herself, with my encouragement, and one afternoon she stayed late and showed me the way to her apartment. It was somewhat awkward at first. Tanya's mom, Cynthia, wasn't sure about me. However before I left, Tanya, Cynthia and I had shared concerns about Tanya's worries (and her spunkiness) and I had shared information about the Battered Womens' emergency phone line and shelter. Although Cynthia minimized the possible need, we identified two people in the apartment building where Tanya could go if Bill ever did come again and she was afraid. We got Cynthia's permission for Tanya to have lunch with me occasionally, and checked out other people in this family's Network that it was OK for Tanya to talk with - and others that Cynthia herself could turn to.

This one doesn't have a fairy tale ending. Bill is invited back sometimes and Tanya, though she's able to keep herself physically safe, is having to face the harsh reality that she can't keep her mom from being hurt. We all learn this sooner or later - most of us have people we love who are not taking as good care of themselves as we'd like them to.

Tanya has decided that school is a safe place and tells us that she sometimes uses math assignments to help her concentrate 'so hard the movies in my head stop.' She also has reported imagining rainbows all around her body as a way of feeling safer and 'outlighting the movies.' She hugs me in the hall, has lunch with me occasionally, stops by to show me a perfect math paper, or to cry sometimes.

A while ago, she came by with a friend.

> 'Ashti needs to talk to you Peg. She has the same problem with her mother that I used to have.'

<u>Used</u> to have?!

>Incident from Schenk Elementary School
>Madison, Wisconsin USA
>October 1982 (Children's names protected)

One of the things we have learned in Protective Behaviours is that sometimes what is helpful for children (and our inner Kidselves) is not what grown-ups or professionals assume will be helpful. As adults we tend to forget, for instance, that being believed and having our perceptions validated is an important life-affirming gift for a child (or anyone) to receive. Adult survivors have told us that this one thing - someone who believed them, and who let them know that they knew what was happening was terrible - was what kept them from complete despair. They have reported this to be true even if that adult was not able to do anything to stop the abuse. Much abuse (all?) starts with a denial of another's perception. I feel that when we believe another's perceptions, this starts to lessen the effect of the abuse. Of course I don't think this is <u>enough</u> - but it is certainly something we can easily, and immediately, give.

....

'Whose hand is this?'

There's a story going the rounds: A woman, going home after a day's work, was tired, so she just sat down in the closest available seat on the bus. The man next to her immediately squeezed up against her. She pulled away. He moved closer, keeping body contact. She tried to ignore him, but he moved his hand next to her thigh, then on it. She stiffened and started to brush his hand away angrily. Then suddenly instead she grabbed his wrist, and holding his hand high above his head, she stood up.

> 'Whose hand is this?' she loudly asked the bus at large. 'I found it on my leg.' And then she moved to another seat.

> -told at a Chimera Self Defense Training
> Madison, Wisconsin, USA November 1987

....

My own best friend

Remembering to be gentle when looking at changing our own habits is vital also. Gwen Flynn, a school principal in New South Wales, Australia commented to me that she started feeling safe and powerful in her life when she began to internalize ... (awareness of the child within) ... and to act on the concept 'I will treat myself as I would treat my best friend.'

....

Cleansing of Iscariot silver

> 'I'm Pastor Norton,'[24] the young man at my office door introduced himself. 'I'd like to give you a donation.'

He handed me an envelope containing some coins.

---

[24] Not his real name.

'I've just been through a difficult time,' he continued before I had a chance to thank him, 'and I'd like to turn this money over to you to use in your work preventing sexual abuse of children.'

'Thanks,' I said. 'We'll use it for that.'

'Twenty pieces of silver' he went on. 'One of my parishioners - a longtime friend actually - thinks I'm a Judas ... thinks that I betrayed him.'

I was certainly curious.

'Sounds like there's a story behind this,' I mused, fingering the dimes.

'Well,' he offered, 'he's counseled with me quite a lot over the past five years, and recently he described some feelings for his five year old daughter that were disturbing to us both. I counseled and prayed with him, but he started acting on the feelings - fondling her ... and more. It was sexual abuse.'

'I prayed with him and told him that God wanted him to stop ... but he made light of it, saying it wasn't important. So I prayed some more myself and received guidance. I told him that God wanted him to admit this sin and get help. I even suggested some therapists. And I said if he didn't get help, I'd have to report him.'

He was upset.

'But you're a Pastor! You can't do that!'

'Then <u>you</u> do it' I urged.

He didn't ... so I did report it. And soon after, he gave me these twenty pieces of silver - Judas money, he called it. But the way I see it I would have been betraying that little girl if I hadn't acted.' He paused.

'So,' he finished, 'I decided the best thing to do with them was to pass them on to you because you're working to stop that.'

Madison, Wisconsin USA January 1989

....

'Looks to me like she doesn't want to go.'

At one point, while I was living in Madison, Wisconsin, some of the male spectators at University of Wisconsin football games participated in an abusive sexist practice, called 'body-passing'. During a lull in the game, or at half time, young men in the stands would grab a young woman in one of the front rows of the stands and, holding her aloft on their hands, would pass her back over their heads to be carried by many male hands until she reached the top tier of the stadium. There disheveled, clothing in disarray, she would be released to return to her seat amid cheers and laughter. There was considerable unwanted touching, women felt this as abusive, but were expected to be 'good sports', and the practice was referred to in the media, as 'high spirits'.

On one occasion, a group of 'high-spirited' (literally as well as figuratively) fraternity boys were present in a group, and made an initial move to start a young woman up the stands. She resisted, but was about to be overpowered, when a slightly older man seated nearby said loudly,

'It looks to me as if she doesn't want to go.'

This Protective Interruption worked, the young men sheepishly abandoned their plan. The cost was that their attention turned on the man who was jeered at for being a spoil sport.

On another occasion, the other women who were sitting with the targetted woman resisted as a group to interrupt the process. The cost to the resisting women was that they were verbally harassed and lesbian-baited throughout the remainder of the game.

After numerous protests, this practice was named for what it was - sexual harassment and assault. It was outlawed in the mid 1980s. Any spectators who attempted to continue the practice were removed from the stadium.

....

Using one-sep-removed to increase self esteem

Patty Fagan, a teacher attending a Two-Day Intensive Training shared that she sometimes has her students stand with her in front of a mirror and tell themselves positive things they like about themselves.

'But some of them can't do it. They say "stupid", or "looks funny" or "ears too big". Things like that ...' she paused.

Just as I was about to prompt with 'What if ...', she did too.

'What if I asked them to pretend they were someone who loves them a lot, and ask what that person would say?'

Later she wrote -

'You know that One-Step Removed thing we thought of with the mirror? Well, it works! And I can also use it for myself when I need to.'

Madison, Wisconsin
September 1989

....

Taking tests

Following a Two Day Training, one participant wrote:

> Here's an anecdote you may appreciate. The second graders to whom I had taught the basic PB Core Process were going to be taking standardized reading tests the next week, and some of they seemed quite apprehensive. I thought it would be good to do a brainstorm about it.

So I suggested:

> "Suppose someone was about to take a test. The teacher was passing out the papers, all was quiet and suddenly that someone felt very nervous - as if everything they ever knew just flew out the window. What could that person do for themselves to feel calmer and remember what they knew?"

Together we listed some fine ideas.

One boy, Jimmy, raised his hand.

> "You could ask the teacher to let you go outside and look underneath the window for what flew out!"

He cemented a place in my heart with that!'

Bev Doud
McHenry, Illinois USA

....

'I can do hard things.'

Three year old Jackie looked up from her self-chosen task.

> 'This is hard!'

> 'Yes, you're right. It is hard,' acknowledged her older companion. 'And you can do hard things. I know, I've seen you.'

Later, the youngster looked up impishly from another self-set task.

> 'This is hard!'
> 'You're doing <u>another</u> hard thing!' rejoined her companion.

> 'Yeah! I can do hard things!' and she returned, grinning, to her task with renewed confidence.

....

'You'll have to ask her.'

> 'And what does the little girl want?' asked the waiter, addressing the four year old's father.
>
> 'I don't know,' he answered as he settled back to read the newspaper. 'You'll have to ask her.'

....

Re-writing nursery rhymes

Some of the attitudes we take in as children come from oft-repeated traditional rhymes and stories. Unaware, we croon and repeat violent, and sometimes sexist and racist phrases. I remember a moment of startlement late one night when I suddenly listened to what I was singing to one of my drowsy infant sons -

> '... when the bough breaks, the cradle will fall,'

From the tree <u>top</u>! Certainly not a safe nor protective image to be putting loved babies to sleep with! It's a very old song ... loving mothers have been singing it for generations. Does it really matter? (Significance level again.[25]) Yes, I believe strongly that it <u>does</u> matter that we have been desensitized to noticing when we are feeding violent, frightening images into our children's minds. A visitor from outer space would certainly see 'Rock-A-Bye Baby' as a hostile song.

The Protective Behaviours Association of South Australia decided to do something about this - they held a contest to re-write nursery rhymes. What a fine example of activity at the Self Level on the Compost Heap!

Thus encouraged, I re-wrote Rock A Bye Baby.

> Rock-a-bye baby, warm by the fire.
> Rocked by a mother, who is ve-ry tired.
> When the babe sleeps, the mother can too
> But now she is rocking the babe fro and to.

And then others joined in. It is contagious, creative kidself fun. We've started using re-writing nursery rhymes as an activity in parent and pre-school staff training groups. Here are ones that some of us in the Wisconsin Network wrote

> Little Miss Muffet sat on a tuffet
> Eating her curds and whey
> Along came a spider and sat down beside her
> To wish her a friendly 'G'day!'

....

---

[25] See *Compost Heap* model of discounting in Chapter 6.

There was a wise woman who lived in a shoe
She lived with lots of children 'cause that's what she liked to do
She gave them Vegemite[26] on buttered bread
Then hugged each one gently and tucked them in bed.

Humpty Dumpty sat on the wall
Trying to decide on which side to fall
Fathers, psychologists, shrinks and all
Couldn't get Humpty to get off the wall

....

Peter, Peter, woman beater
Had a wife and tried to keep her
Her sisters came and they did yell
And Sarah no more with him doth dwell

....

Differently-abled mice, differently-abled mice,
They phoned up and met with the stingy ones
Insisting on access and adequate funds
Nearly impossible things were done
By the differently-abled mice

Do some yourself!

Try Again Red Riding Hood[27] is an example of what happens when we invite children to re-write fairy tales into more self-empowering forms using Protective Behaviours ideas.

What if ... Little Red Riding Hood learns Protective Behaviours ...?

What if ...there could be a different ending than the wolf getting his head cut off? We've never liked that part of the story ...

What if ... Little Red Riding Hood taught Protective Behaviours to Granny?

Self-empowerment in action. In writing this book, the children at Surrey Downs Primary School, South Australia were aided and abetted by their teacher, Helen Monro and Essence Editors, Sue Gordon and Sandy Litt.

....

---

26 Non-Australian readers unfamiliar with this delicacy can substitute a suitably nostalgic childhood food of their own choosing!

27 Try Again Red Riding Hood. *Helen Munro and Children of Surrey Downs Primary School.* Essence Publications. Adelaide, 1989.

Thirty thousand dollars worth of risking on purpose!

We were sitting in the Bank Manager's office, the paperwork completed. We had the loan - and $30,000 worth of good reasons to have our Early Warning Signs. But what did we do? We walked out of that office and gave each other a big hug.

How had we reached this point?

Sue Gordon, not a risk taker by nature and Sandy Litt a gambler with anything except money, overjoyed at the prospect of being $30,000 in debt. Yes, how our lives have changed since being involved in Protective Behaviours.

About two years ago, we had a bright idea - to create stories that would illustrate the Protective Behaviours ideas for young children. The idea grew and grew ... and grew. Our initial plan was simply to give the stories to teachers who were already using the PB Programme with preschoolers. Once the stories were written we thought it would be a good idea to get them illustrated. When we saw the illustrations we realized that Sharon Brooks, our illustrator, had breathed life into our characters and knew that the resulting books needed to be made more widely available than we'd originally envisioned.

With some trepidation we sent our manuscripts to Peg Flandreau West. Without her support for *The Gillows of Crimpley Creek* and *The Troggs of Wongo-Wongo Wood*,[28] we would have been reluctant to continue. However her encouragement and enthusiasm was far beyond our greatest expectations.

Our transition from authors to entrepreneurs had begun. Our first step, we thought, was to find a publisher - a step we both felt safe with. But it did not work. Some driving force within us said,

'Why not publish yourselves?'

Our self talk responded,

'We know nothing about publishing and we both have full time jobs.'

Yet our inner selves had learnt about the Persistence Expectation, and Protective Behaviours is all about saying 'I can!' not 'I can't.'

And so we did - but cautiously at first.

Not ready at this stage to risk our own money, and not having enough to risk anyway, we started to approach potential sponsors. Our hopes high, we compiled a list. By this time the Persistence Expectation was second nature to us, and it needed to be!

---

[28] *Nolly and Groffle the Gillows of Crimpley Creek* and *Zing and Zipp the Troggs of Wongo Wongo Wood*, both by Sue Gordon and Sandy Litt. Essence Publications. Adelaide. 1988.

It took nearly a year before the message sank through that we needed to take another risk. Everyone we spoke to was extremely supportive of our ideas but nobody was prepared to put their money where their mouths were. It finally dawned on us that we would have to take another risk and raise money ourselves.

To raise enough money to publish the books was out of the question. Then the brilliant idea of first creating posters was born. We were able to finance the printing of these ourselves, with a little help from family members. The posters sold so well we took an even bigger risk, and so did the Bank Manager. Which brings us back to where this story began.

It is now several months since the launch of the books. (To have Peg participate in that launch in May 1988 was our great delight!) We have already sold more than 25% of our first printing of 10,000 books, and are about to go into a second print of posters. This has all happened with minimal publicity.

Most of our sales so far have been within our own state of South Australia, but word is spreading to other states. We have now sold some of our products in the USA, and have just received our first New Zealand order.

Things are going so well that it is time to take the next risk. We need to reduce our working hours in our other jobs in order to promote our books and posters more widely. And we are ready to start writing the other books which we have already planned in our heads.

Our initial partnership, Essence Publications, is about to be transformed into a company - Essence Publications Pty, Ltd.

Where to next, we wonder? Finding out will be an adventure.

> Excerpt from a letter
> Sue Gordon and Sandy Litt
> Authors, among other things,
> Essence Publications Pty Ltd, South Australia
> August 1988.

CHAPTER 10

WHAT DO YOU CALL THE LAST CHAPTER WHEN YOU DON'T WANT TO CALL IT AN EPILOGUE?

CAN WE STILL CALL IT 'LOOKING FORWARD'?

Editor's note:

In my various communications with Peg West over the publication of this book, one consistent comment made by both Peg and myself was that it needed a final chapter - we called it a 'Looking Forward Statement'.

That chapter was never written, and for me to write a 'Looking Forward Statement" when the author and subject of the book is no longer with us in physical form might seem a little strange. The alternative of calling it an epilogue didn't quite fit either, because it sounds like an ending and Peg West's story has not ended, in fact it may only just have begun.

What the 'ending' will be depends on each one of us who cares about the future of our world and the safety of all who dwell in it. Each one of us can play a part in bringing about a non-violent future. Each one of us can write our own 'looking forward statement' if we choose to do so.

So let us finish this book, but not the Peg West story, with some of Peg's words. For those readers who did not know the person of Peg Flandreau West, may these words be an encouragement to join an extended network of which each one can be a member.

....

I've recently developed what I sometimes call Shiva Networks. Shiva, you may recall is an Indian diety with several sets of arms. Mike Adams, on one of my visits to Tasmania, suggested that Shiva might be a good choice as patron saint for Protective Behaviours because of the potential for many hand networks.[29] Glenn Halak had also suggested this earlier on. At the present writing I'm aware of having purposely formed numerous networks to support risking and adventures in various aspects of my life - adventures in prosperity thinking and acting, and physical wellness support, for example.

---

[29] One of the graphics we use to teach the Protective Behaviours network concept is a hand tracing. The thumb represents the givens - the grown-ups at home, while the fingers are initialled with four individually selected people other than household members.

I now have a network for financial risking. There are network people I can call when finances get tight and my worry voice starts obsessing about getting a 'real job.' People on this Network support prosperity thinking and trust in the future. They help me protectively interrupt collapsing back into the rational-logical old paradigm thinking. Some of them recently supported me in contracting to buy a new car.

'Of course you need a reliable car. Go for it.'

And they celebrate with me each month when I again meet the monthly car payment. Recently they supported me when I was exploring getting a home equity loan in order to have time to complete this book.

'Of course that's an investment in your future - probably the best thing you can do right now with that money.'

'It's an act of faith in yourself. Do it!'

And my friend, Nancy Livingston, needs only a hint to exhort me -

'Don't you dare get a "regular" job! You have a _cause_ to attend to.'

I also now have a wellness workout network of several people who work out, walk and exercise with me - with noticeable results in suppleness, increased energy and muscles. Many fantasies get shared, hatching numerous ideas and plans as we row, bicycle side by side at different speeds on stationary bikes, lift weights, or stride along on the treadmills or beside the lake, weather permitting.

The widespread Protective Behaviours Network, which has been so central to my life since 1984, now has so many facets! Although many of us do not have a geographical collectiveness, and all at times experience the tyranny of distance,[30] I am continually aware of others' work, plerk and support. I now feel that I never do anything alone, but have the experience and connections of many, many people - even when I am sitting alone in my office writing. Perhaps especially when I am sitting alone with my computer giving words to my latest thoughts - thoughts that for the rest of my life will reflect the clarifications and insights of many of you now reading these words.

Not infrequently, my Inner Elder, Old Peg, convenes a Council of Elders, some of whom I recognize as past forces in my life, and some of whom I don't (yet?) recognize. Whatever, this group of attentive spirits is lending a supportive and comforting dimension to my life, risks and decisions at this time. Perhaps others of you have similar connections. All networks do not live in human bodies!

---

[30] Tyranny of distance - a particularly evocative phrase I first heard from friends in Australia.

ESSENCE PUBLICATIONS are specialists in Protective Behaviours and other child protection resource materials.

BOOKS

Zing and Zipp: The Troggs of Wongo Wongo Wood - Beautifully illustrated stories for primary school children which reinforce the main concepts of Protective Behaviours.

Nolly and Groogle: The Gillows of Crimpley Creek - Beautifully illustrated stories for preschoolers to introduce the ideas of feeling safe and talking about feelings.

Try Again Red Riding Hood - An activity book for primary school children, written and illustrated by 9 year olds, helps children to develop their problem solving skills.

Trust Your Feelings - A resource manual for primary school teachers that contains hundreds of ideas for integrating Protective Behaviours into the junior and lower primary school curriculum. Includes nearly 70 worksheets.

Listen! - A powerful and moving anthology of poetry and prose written by women and men whose children have been sexually abused.

The Basic Essentials - The Protective Behaviours Training Manual by Peg Flandreau West. Available from Protective Behaviours State Groups in Australia.

Safe Adventurous and Loving - A booklet for parents by Peg Flandreau West which outlines five simple steps to help children keep safe.

POSTERS

Theme Posters - 4 colourful Posters (600 x 420mm) stating the themes We all have the right to feel safe all the time and Nothing is so awful that you can't talk to someone about it.

Speak-Out Poster - Safe - Belinda Grant's winning entry in SPEAK OUT 1990. Excellent for survivors of abuse.

AUDIO TAPE

Feeling Safe - A cassette of 9 songs incorporating Protective Behaviours concepts for young children.

For catalogue and price list, information about the Protective Behaviours program and details of new publications contact:

ESSENCE PUBLICATIONS PTY LTD
P.O. BOX 228, BURNSIDE, SOUTH AUSTRALIA 5066 PHONE (08) 31 5326